THE LEAD GUIDE
FOR
SOCIAL RESPONSIBILITY

Creating a new and powerful organization

by Norman Bodek
assisted by Ahmed Avais and Christophe Makni

The Leader's Guide for Social Responsibility

PCS Press

Vancouver, Washington

PCS Inc.
PCS Press
809 S.E. 73rd Avenue
Vancouver, WA 98664
1-360-737-1883

bodek@pcspress.com
http://www.pcspress.com

Printed in the United States of America
Printing number
1 2 3 4 5 6 7 8 9 10

The cover is a stereogram designed by Gene Levine
Library of Congress Cataloging-in-publication Data

p. cm.
Includes index.

ISBN 978-0-9845565-4-0
1. Human development. 2. Industrial Management.
3. Organizational change. 4. Organizational behavior.
5. Human relations.

Dedication

I dedicate this book to my wife, Noriko Hosoyamada, a doctor of Chinese Medicine. I appreciate her medical skill, her amazing cooking ability; truly a great chef, her ability to keep things in order, her support and her patience in fully tolerating the "crazy" things I do.

I want to thank Todd Michael Altstadt for his assistance in checking the references cited, to Gene Levine for designing the cover, to Ahmed Avais and Christophe Makni for their assistance in creating this book and in designing the social responsibility workshop. Also, I thank Paul Akers, John Bernard, Kazuo Inamori, Christophe Makni, and Kazuyoshi Hisano for their very interesting material.

ii **Creating a new and powerful organization**

Foreword

"God does not make mediocre people. God makes only geniuses." - Lou Tice

Because of the pandemic coronavirus, as I write this, we are going through a health crisis which could be the most challenging moment for us since World War II. Over 2,472,062 people, worldwide, have been affected, 170,133 died, close to 20 million Americans out of work, with Industry shutting down, restaurants are closed, public events are closed, schools are closed, borders are shut down; we are told to stay home; millions more could die, and our future seems to look bleak.

It is bad, tragic; our political leaders have handled this very badly by not anticipating our medical needs. But humankind has gone through all kinds of disasters in the past and we have survived.

"The State Department on Thursday issued an extraordinary advisory urging Americans not to travel overseas and to return to the United States if they can, a move that comes amid concerns about the coronavirus pandemic.

The Level 4 travel advisory for all international travel appears to be unprecedented and is the most severe such warning issued by the department."

Creating a new and powerful organization

Symbolically, Phoenix[1] rises out from the ashes and allows us to make a better world as we rise out of this virus confrontation. Yes, it is a bad time for us, an unexpected very bad time, but I want you to also see this as an opportunity for us to change our past behavior. It can be an opportunity to create a new and exciting world. It can be a new opportunity to improve the quality of work life for others and for yourself.

My wife Noriko is reading a Japanese book, *Road to Success that Brings Miracles to Your Life*, by Yasushi Ohno, printed in 2016, he states that enormous changes will happen in the world in 2020. Ohno writes that for the past 3000 years people have been led by leaders, rulers, but that the year 2020 will bring a new world where people will become more autonomous and start to learn how to rule themselves. This is amazing!

Last year, 2019, 181 of the top 200 CEO's in America, members of the Business Roundtable, made a new

---

[1] Phoenix, a mythical bird from Greek and Roman legends, represents transformation, death, and rebirth in its fire. As a powerful spiritual totem, the phoenix is the ultimate symbol of strength and renewal.

commitment to have their organizations become more socially responsible to serve their customers better, to serve their employees better through training and skill building, to have better relationships with their suppliers, to be more concerned with their communities and the environment and also to think more long-term to serve their investors well. Look, the trick is to improve social responsibility and still remain successful. We know that you can do it.

This is a dynamic shift from the past focus almost exclusively on profits. We applaud and welcome this important change at this momentous time.

We will surely get through this virus pandemic and this new commitment from America's corporate leaders allows us to look freshly at how we do business. What is the purpose of our company? Why are we in business? I believe the leader now should become a coach focused on helping people to develop themselves and to really become more autonomous.

In the past, it might have been profits only for the shareholders, but that did not give much excitement to most of us. Yes, work should be a place that fulfills us, a happy experience, a place where we can grow our skills and capabilities, make a nice living and also to serve others.

Prior to 1900, people were fundamentally farmers or highly skilled trades people. Then along comes Frederick Taylor and Henry Ford with the simplification of work. Skill is virtually gone; people on the assembly line doing boring repetitive tasks. Ford from the new system became one of the most successful companies in the world and a model for every other company. We dehumanized work and the

companies became rich. However, few people had choices.
They needed the work to make a living.

Strangely, maybe we can view the virus as a good
thing if it gets us to change the very nature of work and to
get us more focused on creating a better world for us all.
People are capable of doing amazing things. They only need
capable managers to help them discover and develop the
talent within them.

We have been destroying this precious earth and
maybe the virus is shouting back at us to "stop." Here in this
book you will see wonderful examples of what companies
are doing to help and stop the hurt.

Of course, you need profits to survive. But we feel
you can do both good, be more socially responsible, improve
your value to your customers and also sustain your profits.

The author of this book has over 40 years' experience
studying the world's best companies, published over 250
management books, 100 were Japanese translations from
great geniuses including Taiichi Ohno and Shigeo Shingo,
creators of the Toyota Production System (LEAN), ran close
to 100 conferences each with an America CEO as keynote,
learned from and met with W. Edwards Deming, Joseph
Juran, Phil Crosby and dozens of other great American
management Gurus, and also ran the first Kaizen Blitz[2] at
Jake Brake, a Danner Company, etc.

---

[2] Danaher prior to the Kaizen Blitz had sales of around two billion dollars. They
did 17.91 billion in 2019.

To lead this change effort, I first want you to recognize that almost everyone is a "*creature of habits*," living in their "*comfort zone*," and almost every person resists going beyond self-imposed barriers. Please recognize those limitations are only self-created and that we all, with effort, can go beyond them. We are here to help you.

We live in a comfort zone where we feel somewhat safe and in control. We often fear going beyond the unknown, the comfort zone. In most companies, there is very little job security. You can easily be laid off or fired if you make a mistake. But when we set ourselves a very high goal, become determined to attain it and are willing to learn new skills to take us there, we almost automatically expand our comfort zone.

This book is a leader's guide to help your organization become more socially responsible. If you can, we recommend you read this book within groups; ask one person to read a chapter and lead the discussions on how you can take the information presented here and apply it in your organization. Reading a book can be helpful but the book only contains information. You need to take that information and apply it.

Of course, you still need profits, without them the company will not survive, but solely focusing on profits has been the demise of many organizations and the world has suffered enormously.[3] What you find in this book, you might already know but were unable to do. Now you have a new mandate. It is up to you to find the best way to accomplish it. **We recommend you just do the right thing!** You know

---

[3] Boeing is an example where management decided to save money on making the 737 Max using an old design instead of a new more costly one. Focusing solely on profits has lost Boeing billions of dollars.

what is right. You know how to treat your customers, your employees, your suppliers and how to improve the environment. Yes, you want to treat others just the way you want to be treated.

We hope as you go through this change process that you will treat your employees better: give them more autonomy[4], encourage them to be more creative, help them learn new skills, offer them meaningful work to do; and challenge them to aspire to grow without limit.

I hope this is a new wonderful journey for us all as we create a better world to live in.

---

[4] Autonomy - American Airlines this week had 11 people on a plane, virus has reduced people flying; they put all 11 in the back of the plane not allowing them to be separated. Yes, the flight attendants were following the rules created by their leaders, not being autonomous and doing the right things.

Table of Contents

Introduction

The Leader's Guide for Social Responsibility

Creating a new and powerful organization

"Geniuses are ordinary people who have had nothing subtracted from them." - Abraham Maslow

In the past fifty years within large corporations, CEO's and their managers have almost been solely committed to producing "profits only." In August 2019, 181 top managers out of the top 200 corporations, members of the Business Roundtable, signed a new commitment to become socially responsible and to serve all "stakeholders,"(customers, employees, suppliers, community/environment, and shareholders,) better.

"Wow," what an amazing commitment! "Wow," what an amazing new opportunity for all managers - for all employees! Think of what this means to you? Think of what this means to our country and the world. It is a positive step in the right direction.

Now, we accept the sincerity of these executives, but we also feel that they do want those profits, at the least the same and even more. The challenge for you is to be able to do it; to be more socially responsible and to sustain profits. Without profits, an organization cannot survive, but also the earth cannot survive if neglected.

2 Sustaining profits and doing the right thing!

Since most managers, in these past 50 years have been focusing on profits, it might not be that easy to make this significant shift. We intend this book to be a guide to help you do, "What is right?" You know what is right! But your hands have been tied. Now, you have a new opportunity to do what is right for all stakeholders: customers, employees, suppliers, community and your shareholders.

We feel that you can be more socially responsible and even to sustain your profits. Surely, customers will pay for value; employees that are taught new skills will create additional value; better relationships with suppliers can reduce costs, add to innovation and add value; the community and the environment dearly needs this shift and will support you; and the shareholders will benefit.

This book is filled with ideas to help you succeed successfully on this new journey. These ideas come from some of the best leaders, managers, consultants, and teachers, from throughout the world. As you read, just pick those ideas you like and feel capable of using. Take notes as your read or just underline. Then relook at them, share them with your associates, add to them and then select the best ones to get you started.

Imagine, envision, how the future can be for you and your organization. As a first step, write what you would like to see in the future of your organization that benefits all stakeholders. And as you read the book, use a check list and enter those items that you would like to implement to create your new company:

Idea	Now	Soon	Later
1. Learn how to ask customers	6-1		
2. Set up a mistake board	6-3		
3. Get a coach		8-1	
4. Review our Lean process			9-1
5.			
6.			
7.			
8.			

Create a great future:

"1. Imagine that you are already living in the future whereby you have already succeeded in delivering the new vision to be socially responsible.

2. Have complete faith and trust in your staff and yourself that you have the skill, or you will acquire it to do the job right.

3. Get involved with more people. Be with people who are already there." - Kazuyoshi Hisano, author of the new book, "CEO Coaching Theory of Thinking and Action to Increase Annual Sales by 100 Times," to be published in English this fall.

4   Sustaining profits and doing the right thing!

"Let me propose a few changes"

Change is not easy

Chapter I - A New Beginning

A significant, historical, shift is taking place in American industry. For the past 50 years large American corporations have focused primarily on making profits virtually ignoring the social needs of our society. But a new spark has been ignited by **Lawrence Douglas Fink, an** American financial executive, chairman and CEO of BlackRock, an American multinational investment management corporation. BlackRock is the largest money-management firm in the world with more than $7.4 trillion in assets under management.

Larry Fink | BlackRock
blackrock.com

In 2018, Mr. Fink wrote to his clients and told them that they must now become socially responsible. **On August 19, 2019, they responded. The Business Roundtable issued an open letter titled** "Statement on the Purpose of a

Corporation." One of the preeminent business lobbies in the United States, the Business Roundtable (BR) includes the CEOs of leading U.S. companies from Apple to Walmart. 181 signatures out of the top 200 CEO's in America wrote a one-page declaration that ended as follows: "Each of our stakeholders is essential. We commit to deliver value to all of them, for the future success of our companies, our communities and our country."

"While each of our individual companies serves its own corporate purpose, we share a fundamental commitment to all of our stakeholders. We commit to:

- **Delivering value to our customers.** We will further the tradition of American companies leading the way in meeting or exceeding customer expectations.
- **Investing in our employees.** This starts with compensating them fairly and providing important benefits. It also includes supporting them through training and education that help develop new skills for a rapidly changing world. We foster diversity and inclusion, dignity and respect.
- **Dealing fairly and ethically with our suppliers.** We are dedicated to serving as good partners to the other companies, large and small, that help us meet our missions.
- **Supporting the communities in which we work.** We respect the people in our communities and protect the environment by embracing sustainable practices across our businesses.
- **Generating long-term value for shareholders**, who provide the capital that allows companies to invest, grow and innovate. We are committed to transparency and effective engagement with shareholders.

Each of our stakeholders is essential. We commit to deliver value to all of them, for the future success of our companies, our communities and our country." - Business Roundtable

Our goal in this book is to help all leaders and managers to fulfill this new commitment.

8 Sustaining profits and doing the right thing!

Chapter II - A new destiny for American Industry

"We are trapped by our habits and ways of doing things and we cannot change our ideas and our actions" - Taiichi Ohno, former VP Manufacturing Toyota and creator of the Toyota Production System

What role do we play in the community? How are we managing our impact on the environment? Are we working to create a diverse workforce? Are we adapting to technological change? Are we providing the retraining and opportunities that our employees and our businesses will need to adjust to an increasingly automated world? Are we using behavioral finance and other tools to prepare workers for retirement, so that they invest in a way that will help them achieve their goals?

Please answer the above questions. Your answers might not be that positive, but that is all about to change.

Hold your breath! Hang on to your seat! Something monumental is happening!

This latest news, we believe will transform the earth for the better. Believe it or not! US Corporations are about to change their fundamental philosophy **from being concerned only about profits,** return to shareholders**, to become socially responsible**, to foster better relationships with their customers; to train and develop their employees as real assets not just as something easily disposable; to have closer ties and have a deeper more positive relationship with their suppliers; to look differently and more responsibly at their community and the environment; along with a continuation to return profits to shareholders.

Centered on profits has made some large corporations tremendously rich but the benefits have not "trickled down" to the rest of us. I am grateful, with sincerity from the top, that this is about to change. It is vitally necessary for top executives and corporations to do this. We cannot expect that much from our government which today is grappling not too successfully with the virus.

The purpose of this book is to help you the leader, the manager, the supervisor, the executive to swiftly, "do the right thing," and help your companies become socially responsible. We need you! You can do it!

I once wrote to Najeeb E. Halaby, the CEO of Pan Am, with a suggestion addressing a problem I had flying on his airplanes. He sent me back a personal handwritten note: ***"Norman, I know exactly what to do to address this problem that people like you are having with us, but I really don't know how to get it done with my staff."*** To me it was a very sad note.

Pan Am was a great airline that went out of business, unable to serve their customer's needs.   This radical *"awakening"* by the leading CEO's in America gives us a new opportunity to give our society a brighter future and to actually save the world.

You want to learn the lesson and not be like Pan Am.

We intend to explain the importance of this new commitment and what it could possibly mean to you personally, to our society, to the world itself, and also offer direction on how you can actually do it. It is often, "easier said than done." After 50 years of primarily pursuing profits only, it will not be easy to live up to their new commitments to become more socially responsible and also to attain their profits.

Survival of the organization is a prime importance, without it everything else is lost. Profits are vital, but we also need to be socially responsible so that at the same time your customers, employees, suppliers and the community also succeeds.

This new commitment requires every manager and supervisor to learn how to be socially responsible. It surely will not be easy for they have been primarily focused on getting those profits. We will give you many ideas to make it work: to

12 Sustaining profits and doing the right thing!

rethink how to serve your customers, to look at employees as real assets, to set up consortiums, partnerships with your suppliers, to create a positive community around you and to also attain the same profits or even more. Look we know you have really good intentions to do this, but we also know you will not reduce your profits. We will help you.

I have had the privilege of working with many of the world's great management masters including Peter Drucker, W. Edwards Deming, Taiichi Ohno, Dr. Shigeo Shingo and many more. I have published over 250 management books, 100 are Japanese translated to English and I have written eight. I have met dozens of CEO's from our top corporations, lectured to over 100 last year at a Chief Executive Net conference in Columbus, Ohio and I have taught management at Portland State University. I have also led over 500 senior American executives on study missions to Japan. My credentials include:

Old me:

- Educated at University of Wisconsin, New York University, New York University Graduate School of Business, and Graduate School of Education
- Two years in the US Army and six years in reserve

- Practiced as a public accountant - Actually, was the first person to automate accounting on a Bendix G15 computer in 1960
- VP at Tape Accounting Center, foolishly refused to take 7% from ADP for our company
- Opened offshore data processing companies in Barbados and in Grenada, West Indies and converted ATT manual records to the computer
- 1979 Started Productivity Inc. - Productivity Press
- Nominated into Industry Week's Hall of Fame
- Nominated into American Manufacturing Association's Hall of Fame
- Listed as one of 50 quality gurus -
  https://tinyurl.com/y4glqqn5
- Started the Shingo Prize at Utah State University
- Consultant on Lean and Kaizen
- Board member of Vantec Inc.

New me:

- Keynoted around 50 management conferences
- Currently teaching "how to set and attain goals"

My teacher Rudi once said, **"Norman, you should have only one wish and that is to grow."** Every day I do look deeply within myself and ask to grow. This is a wish that everyone should ask, to keep growing to reach their maximum creative ability. Imagine, how great our corporations would be if everyone working for them were improving their skills and reaching always to be better - reaching to a level of mastery. To do this, we need a new vision from the organization to serve our society better and to give people the inspiration necessary to support that vision through their individual growth.

"A great leader knows his own insufficiencies and never thinks during his whole life that he has succeeded."

Work should be exciting! When getting up in the morning, you should look forward to going to work. This is the challenge of managers to help people find work exciting.

The new commitment from the 181 CEO's is wonderful and it is also contagious as other organizations are starting to support it, but change is not easy. Can the corporations deliver on their new commitments and also attain their shareholder value - their profits? We hope to show you how.

Every manager and every supervisor will now have a new role to go from controllers, from bosses, to focusing almost exclusively on developing people to their maximum capability. People are your most important asset and must be treated that way.

In 1970, Milton Friedman, noble prize winner, in his Friedman Doctrine, or Shareholder Theory, held that a firm's main responsibility is to its shareholders. This approach views shareholders as the economic engine of the organization and the only group to which the firm is socially responsible. As such, the goal of the firm is to maximize returns to shareholders. Friedman argued that the shareholders can then decide for themselves what social initiatives to take part in, rather than have an executive the shareholders appointed explicitly for business purposes decide for them.

During the last 50 years, the leaders of many top corporations have done a fantastic job in delivering profits.[5] Some of them are even bigger economically than many countries. Apple, Inc.'s net worth is 750 billion dollars. Apple is worth more than the value of 171 countries out of over 200 countries in the world. only 29 countries are richer than Apple. Just 9 of the world's richest men have more combined wealth than the poorest 4 billion people. Bill Gates has more money than the national wealth of 38 different countries.

And the CEO's have been substantially rewarded for their success. In 1970, the average CEO earned around 20 times more than the average worker. Today it is closer to 300 times, averaging around 18.6 million dollars, some even reaching 100 million.

---

[5] In 1960, Fortune listed the 500 top corporations in America, only 60 are independent today. They surely are highly successful. Oops, HP is close to leaving the list.

16 Sustaining profits and doing the right thing!

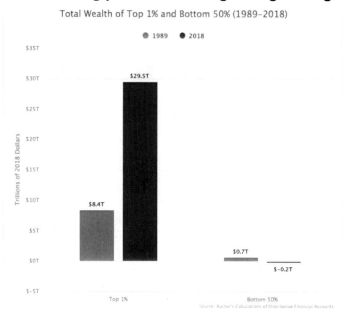

Total Wealth of Top 1% and Bottom 50% (1989–2018)

● 1989 ● 2018

"A recent analysis of a Federal Reserve report found between 1989 and 2018, the top 1 percent increased its total net worth by $21 trillion. The bottom 50 percent actually saw its net worth decrease by $900 billion over the same period."
- June 24, 2019

What kind of world were we creating?

While these corporations have been earning huge profits, unfortunately, the stockholders receiving these great profits have not been that altruistic in helping the world also benefit from their success. The earth has suffered substantially. Millions of species have disappeared, plastic is killing our oceans and all the life therein is threatened.

Carbon has polluted our skies causing untold illnesses; weather has been hotter than previous, the ice caps are melting, and the oceans are rising with hurricanes and other storms increasing. If we continued to pursue profits before everything else, life on earth shortly will disappear.

Our hero Lawrence Douglas Fink in his 2018 annual open letter to CEOs, called for corporations to play an active role in improving the environment, working to better their communities, and increasing the diversity of their workforces. This has been taken as evidence of a move by Blackrock, one of the largest public investors, to proactively enforce these targets. In his 2018 open letter Fink said that companies and their CEOs must step into a leadership vacuum to tackle social and political issues when governments fail to address these issues." - https://en.wikipedia.org/wiki/Laurence_D._Fink

The following comes from his statement. To read the entire statement go to: https://tinyurl.com/snwm2q9

"Dear CEO,

As BlackRock approaches its 30th anniversary this year, I have had the opportunity to reflect on the most pressing issues facing investors today and how BlackRock must adapt to serve our clients more effectively.

We are seeing a paradox of high returns and high anxiety. Since the financial crisis, those with capital have reaped enormous benefits. At the same time, many individuals across the world are facing a combination of low rates, low wage growth, and inadequate retirement systems. Many don't have the financial capacity, the resources, or the tools to save effectively; those who are invested are too often over-allocated to cash. For millions, the prospect of a secure retirement is slipping further and further away – especially among workers with less education, whose job security is increasingly tenuous. I believe these trends are a major source of the anxiety and polarization that we see across the world today.

We also see many governments failing to prepare for the future, on issues ranging from retirement and infrastructure to automation and worker retraining. As a result, society increasingly is turning to the private sector and asking that companies respond to broader societal challenges. Indeed, the public expectations of your company have never been greater. Society is demanding that companies, both public and private, serve a social purpose. To prosper over time, every company must not only deliver financial performance, but also show how it makes a positive contribution to society. Companies must benefit all of their stakeholders, including shareholders, employees, customers, and the communities in which they operate…

Without a sense of purpose, no company, either public or private, can achieve its full potential. It will ultimately lose the license to operate from key stakeholders. It will succumb to short-term pressures to distribute earnings, and, in the process, sacrifice investments in employee development, innovation, and capital expenditures that are necessary for long-term growth.

A new model for corporate governance

… BlackRock can choose to sell the securities of a company if we are doubtful about its strategic direction or long-term growth….

Your strategy, your board, and your purpose

In order to make engagement with shareholders as productive as possible, companies must be able to describe their strategy for long-term growth.

The statement of long-term strategy is essential to understanding a company's actions and policies, its preparation for potential challenges, and the context of its shorter-term decisions. *Your company's strategy must articulate a path to achieve financial performance. To sustain that performance, however, you must also understand the societal impact of your business as well as the ways that broad, structural trends – from slow wage growth to rising automation to climate change – affect your potential for growth...*

Companies must ask themselves: What role do we play in the community? How are we managing our impact on the environment? Are we working to create a diverse workforce? Are we adapting to technological change? Are we providing the retraining and opportunities that our employees and our business will need to adjust to an increasingly automated world? Are we using behavioral finance and other tools to prepare workers for retirement, so that they invest in a way that will help them achieve their goals?

Today, our clients – who are your company's owners – are asking you to demonstrate the leadership and clarity that will drive not only their own investment returns, but also the prosperity and security of their fellow citizens. We look forward to engaging with you on these issues.

Sincerely,

(signature) "

The above statement by Lawrence Fink written in 2018 is a significant and powerful message to America's leading CEO's and we believe is the great catalyst that can and will save the world. It is that momentous!

Business giants worth $16 trillion commit to sustainable investment

The CEOs of 30 global business giants who make up the newly launched Global Investors for Sustainable Development (GISD) Alliance (they manage $16 trillion) recognizes that long-term environmental sustainability and social responsibility are every bit as important as short-term profit.

In their first joint statement, GISD members openly recognized that their "business success is inseparable from sustained, inclusive and sustainable economic development" and committed to a *"long-term approach to business and investment decisions."*

Breaking with stereotypes still held by many investors, the GISD CEOs acknowledged that sustainable development is not incompatible with good business practice. On the contrary, business success and a sustainable future are inextricably linked. Investment in societal development and reduction of inequality creates healthy, educated, and empowered workers and, ultimately, customers—who are vital to growth and prosperity in every business, sector, and industry.

In their joint statement, GISD Alliance members committed to develop innovative financing facilities, establish partnerships and contribute to sustainable economic growth that benefits all stakeholders—not just the shareholders of companies. VOL 23, NO. 11 - NOVEMBER 2019 -

On October 15, 2019 in the New York Times: https://tinyurl.com/y5c8xes2

Marc Benioff: We Need a New Capitalism

Only parts shown:

"Capitalism, I acknowledge, has been good to me.

Over the past 20 years, the company that I co-founded, Salesforce, has generated billions in profits and made me a very wealthy person.

Yet, as a capitalist, I believe it's time to say out loud what we all know to be true: Capitalism, as we know it, is dead.

Yes, free markets — and societies that cherish scientific research and innovation — have pioneered new industries, discovered cures that have saved millions from disease and unleashed prosperity that has lifted billions of people out of poverty. On a personal level, the success that I've achieved has allowed me to embrace philanthropy and invest in improving local public schools and reducing homelessness in the San Francisco Bay Area, advancing children's health care and protecting our oceans.

22 Sustaining profits and doing the right thing!

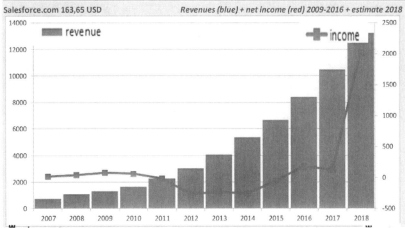

Salesforce.com 163,65 USD   Revenues (blue) + net income (red) 2009-2016 + estimate 2018

But capitalism as it has been practiced in recent decades — with its obsession on maximizing profits for shareholders — has also led to horrifying inequality. Globally, the 26 richest people in the world now have as much wealth as the poorest 3.8 billion people, and the relentless spewing of carbon emissions is pushing the planet toward catastrophic climate change. In the United States, income inequality has reached its highest level in at least 50 years, with the top 0.1 percent — people like me — owning roughly 20 percent of the wealth while many Americans cannot afford to pay for a $400 emergency. It's no wonder that support for capitalism has dropped, especially among young people.

share of wealth in the world

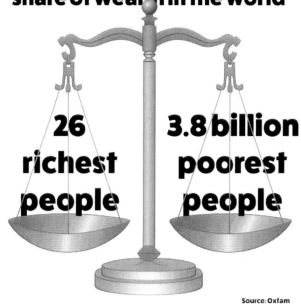

Source: Oxfam

To my fellow business leaders and billionaires, I say that we can no longer wash our hands of our responsibility for what people do with our products. Yes, profits are important, but so is society. And if our quest for greater profits leaves our world worse off than before, all we will have taught our children is the power of greed.

It's time for a new capitalism — a more fair, equal and sustainable capitalism that actually works for everyone and where businesses, including tech companies, don't just take from society but truly give back and have a positive impact.

What might a new capitalism look like?

First, business leaders need to embrace a broader vision of their responsibilities by looking beyond shareholder return and also measuring their stakeholder return. This

Sustaining profits and doing the right thing!

requires that they focus not only on their shareholders, but also on all of their stakeholders — their employees, customers, communities and the planet. Fortunately, nearly 200 executives with the Business Roundtable recently committed their companies, including Salesforce, to this approach, saying that the "purpose of a corporation" includes "a fundamental commitment to all of our stakeholders." As a next step, the government could formalize this commitment, perhaps with the Security and Exchange Commission requiring public companies to publicly disclose their key stakeholders and show how they are impacting those stakeholders.

Unfortunately, not everyone agrees. Some business leaders objected to the landmark declaration. The Council of Institutional Investors argued that 'it is government, not companies, that should shoulder the responsibility of defining and addressing societal objectives." When asked whether companies should serve all stakeholders and whether capitalism should be updated, Vice President Mike Pence warned against "leftist policies.'

But suggesting that companies must choose between doing well and doing good is a false choice. Successful businesses can and must do both. In fact, with political dysfunction in Washington, D.C., Americans overwhelmingly say C.E.O.s should take the lead on economic and social challenges, and employees, investors and customers increasingly seek out companies that share their values.

When government is unable or unwilling to act, business should not wait. Our experience at Salesforce shows that profit and purpose go hand in hand and that business can be the greatest platform for change.

For many businesses, giving back to their communities is an afterthought — something they only do after they've turned a profit. But by integrating philanthropy into our company culture from the beginning — giving 1 percent of our equity, time and technology — Salesforce has donated nearly $300 million to worthy causes, including local public schools and addressing homelessness.

Globally, few nations are meeting their targets to fight climate change, the current United States presidential administration remains determined to withdraw from the Paris Agreement and global emissions continue to rise. As governments fiddle, there are steps that business can take now, while there's still time, to prevent the global temperature from rising more than 1.5 degrees Celsius. Every company can do something, whether reducing emissions in their operations and across their sector, striving for net-zero emissions like Salesforce, moving toward renewable energies or aligning their operations and supply chains with emissions reduction targets.

Skeptical business leaders who say that having a purpose beyond profit hurts the bottom line should look at the facts. Research shows that companies that embrace a broader mission — and, importantly, integrate that purpose into their corporate culture — outperform their peers, grow faster, and deliver higher profits. Salesforce is living proof that new capitalism can thrive, and everyone can benefit. We don't have to choose between doing well and doing good. They're not mutually exclusive. In fact, since becoming a public company in 2004, Salesforce has delivered a 3,500 percent return to our shareholders. Values create value.

Of course, C.E.O. activism and corporate philanthropy alone will never be enough to meet the immense scale of *today's challenges. It could take $23 billion a year to address racial inequalities in our public schools. College graduates are drowning in $1.6 trillion of student debt. It will cost billions to retrain American workers for the digital jobs of the future. Trillions of dollars of investments will be needed to avert the worst effects of climate change. All this, when our budget deficit has already surpassed $1 trillion.*

How, exactly, is our country going to pay for all this?

That is why a new capitalism must also include a tax system that generates the resources we need and includes higher taxes on the wealthiest among us. Local efforts — like the tax I supported last year on San Francisco's largest companies to address our city's urgent homelessness crisis — will help. Nationally, increasing taxes on high-income individuals like myself would help generate the trillions of dollars that we desperately need to improve education and health care and fight climate change.

The culture of corporate America needs to change, and it shouldn't take an act of Congress to do it. Every C.E.O. and every company must recognize that their responsibilities do not stop at the edge of the corporate campus. When we finally start focusing on stakeholder value as well as shareholder value, our companies will be more successful, our communities will be more equal, our societies will be more just, and our planet will be healthier."
https://tinyurl.com/y5c8xes2

Marc Benioff is the chairman and co-chief executive of Salesforce and the author, with Monica Langley, of the forthcoming book, "Trailblazer: The Power of Business as the Greatest Platform for Change."

Well that should "knock" the "socks" off your feet.
It is just great and well needed. In this book, we intend to help you do it. To set new roles for managers and supervisors to allow this dynamic shift to take place.

Look, we are not suggesting that the Corporations and CEO's make less money. In fact, following our suggestions and others we interviewed should allow you to make your profits and at the same time being good to the rest of us.

Simon Sinek's rebuttal:

"Forgive Simon Sinek if he's supportive of the sentiment but skeptical of the sincerity of the Business Roundtable in its recent self-redefinition of the purpose of a corporation, extending it to include the interests of employees, customers and the community as well as the traditional concerns of shareholders.

The business-leadership and work-culture guru, best known for a massively popular TED talk and the bestselling book Start with Why, called the declaration by the group of business leaders, signed by 181 CEOs of major U.S. companies, 'pablum,' 'insufficient' and redolent of 'cheap' talk, questioning the Business Roundtable's motives and whether the statement really will change anything.

'What will change?' Sinek, who shares his philosophy about management and workplace transformation in books and in appearances around the world, tells Chief Executive. 'It's fine to have a statement of generic values that you write on the wall of a company — but what will change? Will these CEOs abandon layoffs as an annual practice to balance their books?'

28 Sustaining profits and doing the right thing!

Sinek wonders 'where is the evidence of conversion' by the signatory CEOs to the point of view expressed by the Business Roundtable statement. One of the signers highlighted by the group, for instance, Jamie Dimon, CEO of JPMorgan Chase, 'just a few years ago announced record-high layoffs, in the exact same year the company announced record-high [executive] bonuses." And marquee signer Alex Gorsky heads Johnson & Johnson, a company that "was just fined $500 million for its involvement in opioids,'

Sinek notes. Rather than operate out of genuine transformation and personal conviction, Sinek speculates, the CEOs who signed the Business Roundtable statement of new principles did so as a result of 'public pressure' that increasingly questions the traditional approach of American corporations, including the popularity of employee-centered approaches such as the one taught by Sinek.

'If they truly believed it, they would have done it 20 years ago ... You're suddenly preaching the cause of people, but you don't just wake up one morning and suddenly believe this,' Sinek says. 'There had to have been some kind of event – and if not, then I don't believe it. I'm curious to see what happens next. Talk is cheap.'

At the same time, Sinek joined the Business Roundtable at least in expressing the view that American capitalism remains the best system for addressing economic inequities, spurring innovation and ensuring growth.

'Even as Adam Smith envisioned it, capitalism is fine,' Sinek says. 'It's just that the brand of [former General Electric CEO Jack Welch] and [the late conservative economist Milton Friedman] is broken. The sole purpose of business isn't to maximize profits – it's to advance society and to offer value.'

He continues, 'The purpose of business is to contribute, and if you're offering something of value that people think enhances life in some shape or form, you'll make a profit. That's how you know you have a viable business – and it's defined by the customer, not the company.'
https://tinyurl.com/yxyn45xc

From Davos:

"Davos elite back corporate social responsibility, but 'their words are bigger than
their actions

- At Davos, politicians and executives will likely talk about 'stakeholder capitalism,' a movement that redefines a company's purpose from serving only its shareholders to all stakeholders, including customers and communities.

- But investors are still holding the strings, according to corporate advisors, investors and experts who spoke to CNBC.

- As some investors are changing their focus toward corporate good, so are companies. But with profit an end goal for most, change has its limits."
https://tinyurl.com/w4z9n2m

An exercise:

The Power of Inquiry (30 – 60 minutes)

30 Sustaining profits and doing the right thing!

Try this with an associate at work; pair two people together and designate them as A and B for ease of instruction below.

Prompt: Think of a challenging issue related to becoming more socially responsible. The more intractable it may seem the better. Now, ask them to take a couple of minutes to write three sentences describing that issue.

i.   A shares what they wrote with B without B interjecting (only listening) (2 minutes – move on to the next step if done earlier)

ii. A remains **silent** and B asks questions. Better to ask open ended questions. Note that it's important for A to remain silent; don't clarify, don't respond. It helps if A writes during that time. (Do this for at least 5 minutes. B must keep asking questions)

iii. A and B discuss and debrief. What new thoughts emerged? What is something you want to remember from this? What do you want to take action on? (3 minutes)

iv. Repeat with A and B roles reversed.

Managers, leaders, can instruct and ask people to do things, but it is much more powerful when people can create their own solutions on their own.

Chapter III - the New Commitment

"You cannot cross the sea merely by standing and staring at the water." – R. Tagore

The purpose of this book is to show how it is possible to be socially responsible while at the same time allow the stockholders to achieve their profits.

Not complicated! **Just do things right!**

"Old way".

"New way"

32 Sustaining profits and doing the right thing!

You surely know right from wrong. Just do things that are good for your customers, your employees, your suppliers, and the environment. Please all stakeholders.

Please write a list of things you can do differently for your organization to become more socially responsible and then add to the list as you read this book. Yes, books can be very helpful, but change requires action - the ability to take the information from the books and apply it.

From Lawrence Fink:

1. What is your purpose in being socially responsible?
2. What role will you take in your community?
3. How will you improve the environment?
4. How will you diverse your workforce?
5. How will you handle technological change?
6. What new training will you give your employees?
7. How will you handle automation?
8. Can you relook at your retirement policies?
9. How will you help your associates set new personal goals for their achievement and also support your organizations vision?

We are writing about being socially responsible and how this can be a very powerful tool for managers and supervisors to create a very new and exciting workplace. Clearly, we should know why the corporation should be socially responsible. We hope you set up discussion groups within to look at this issue deeply. What is the purpose of your corporation? For fifty years it was fundamentally to make a profit for your shareholders, but now it will be different.

Needed also is a very strong vision and a philosophy to inspire and drive forward your new commitment. President Kennedy was famous for stating that within 10 years we would put a man on the moon. HIs vision opened the door to that possibility.

After World War II, Japan was destroyed. In Tokyo, Osaka and Nagoya, *"the areas leveled (almost 100 square miles (260 km) exceeded the areas <u>destroyed</u> in all <u>German</u> cities by both the <u>American</u> and <u>British</u> <u>air</u> <u>forces</u> (approximately 79 square miles (200 km).."* Also, most of their smaller cities were destroyed. My wife Noriko is Japanese and her mother Mitchko told me their hometown of Kokobu was totally leveled after World War II. Miraculously, the Japanese quickly reconstructed. They sent tens of thousands of people to America to study and learn from us. They did learn very well. They came with their camera's and took pictures of anything of value and went back and copied and replicated what they saw.

Japan was noted as a nation of copiers. Their products were "cheap," often called junk. We laughed at them. Toyota around 1960 sent a few hundred automobiles to sell in America and then sent 60 back to be reworked. And yet, Toyota today is one of the largest most successful companies in the world. Yes, Japan copied us but then perfected it and rose quickly to become the second largest industrial nation in the world. Tokyo rose from the "ashes" and now is one of the most modern cities in the world.

34 Sustaining profits and doing the right thing!

On my latest trip to Japan, I asked my wife's beautician, *"how many hours do you work?"* She said, "I work 11 hours six days a week." I visited an acupuncturist and asked the same question, "I start at 9:00am and finish at 9:30pm, six days a week."

In order for the Japanese to catch up to America after World War II, it was necessary for the Japanese worker to work exceptionally long hours. Many people would work from 9:00am to 9:00pm and also often on Saturday. With their intensity in many ways they did catch America but "nobody told them that they made it," for you will see people working those long hours today. My wife is a doctor and is also Japanese and her nephew, a software engineer, leaves his house a little after 6:00am and returns home at around 10:00pm and also will often work on Saturday.

I am not saying that you need to have your workers follow these same long hours, but you must consider what you need to do to stay up to international competition.

Set a vision

In 1946, Koichi Tsukamoto, started a women's lingerie company, later called Wacoal, initially had major financial difficulties and also had problems with their company union. The union wanted more money for the workers, more than he could afford. He thought he would go bankrupt if he gave them more money. He reluctantly gave them the raise; the company survived, and he also wrote a fifty-year vision, broken into 10-year segments to eventually become the world's leader in fine women's lingerie:

1. to be established in Japan,

2. to be known as a premium bra brand known for fit, quality, comfort, and craftsmanship,
3. to be recognized as a leading lingerie company in Japan,
4. to reach out into the world, and
5. to be the best women's lingerie company in the world.

"Wacoal®, today is the leader in designer intimate apparel in the United States, Japan, Asia, and Europe and is internationally known for the best-fitting, highest-quality bras in the world. After nearly two decades of success in America and now officially America's #1 selling bra; Wacoal continues to offer luxurious intimate apparel made from exquisite laces, embroideries, and the finest fabrications, tailored to create the perfect fit. Wacoal spends months developing every bra and panty design, guaranteeing perfection and customer satisfaction. The designs are a combination of European elegance and a comfortable American fit."
https://www.6pm.com/b/wacoal/brand/3304

***Do* it!** Make sure your company has a long-term vision that will align your customers, employees, suppliers, community and your shareholders. Get them all excited about your purpose.

I recommend you write a very strong new vision and mission to balance all that is in front of you and get your team to seriously find ways to stay highly profitable and also ensure that the world will be sustained.

President Kennedy said in 1961:

"I believe that this nation should commit itself to achieving the goal, before this decade is out, of <u>landing a</u>

man on the moon and returning him safely to the Earth. No single space project in this period will be more impressive to mankind, or more important for the long-range exploration of space; and none will be so difficult or expensive to accomplish. We propose to accelerate the development of the appropriate lunar space craft. We propose to develop alternate liquid and solid fuel boosters, much larger than any now being developed, until certain which is superior. We propose additional funds for other engine development and for unmanned explorations, which are particularly important for one purpose which this nation will never overlook: the survival of the man who first makes this daring flight. But in a very real sense, it will not be one _man going to the moon_--if we make this judgment affirmatively, it will be an entire nation. For all of us must work to put him there."
https://www.nasa.gov/vision/space/features/jfk_speech_text.html

His vision inspired the nation and we attained it. I recommend you do the same.

Toyota Motor Corporation's vision statement indicates the company's long-term strategic direction in the automobile industry. This vision statement reads, "_Toyota will lead the way to the future of mobility, enriching lives around the world with the safest and most responsible ways of moving people. Through our commitment to quality, constant innovation and respect for the planet, we aim to exceed expectations and be rewarded with a smile. We will meet our challenging goals by engaging the talent and passion of people, who believe there is always a better way._" https://tinyurl.com/vslaafr

Study the best, yes, copy them and then get better

I recommend you read the vision and mission statements from those you admire. I love the ones I have studied in Japan like Kyocera primarily created by Kazuo Inamori and also, I recommend you study the statements from Konosuke Matsushita who started Panasonic.

Look at Patagonia: 'We're in business to save our home planet.

Our Reason for Being

"At Patagonia, we appreciate that all life on earth is under threat of extinction. We aim to use the resources we have—our business, our investments, our voice and our imaginations—to do something about it.

As the climate crisis deepens, we see a potential, even probable end to such moments, and so we're fighting to save them. We donate our time, services and at least 1 percent of our sales to help hundreds of grassroots organizations all over the world so that they can remain vigilant and protect what's irreplaceable. At the same time, we know that we risk saving a tree only to lose the forest—a livable planet. As the loss of biodiversity, arable soils, coral reefs and fresh water all accelerate, we are doing our best to address the causes, and not just   symptoms, of global warming.

Staying true to our core values during forty-plus years in business has helped us create a company we're proud to run and work for. To stay in business for at least forty more, we must defend the place we all call home.

Core Values

Our values reflect those of a business started by a band of climbers and surfers, and the minimalist style they promoted. The approach we take toward product design demonstrates a bias for simplicity and utility.

Build the best product

Our criteria for the best product rests on function, repairability, and, foremost, durability. Among the most direct ways we can limit ecological impacts is with goods that last for generations or can be recycled so the materials in them remain in use. Making the best product matters for saving the planet.

Cause no unnecessary harm

We know that our business activity—from lighting stores to dyeing shirts—is part of the problem. We work steadily to change our business practices and share what we've learned. But we recognize that this is not enough. We seek not only to do less harm, but do better.

Use business to protect nature

The challenges we face as a society require leadership. Once we identify a problem, we act. We embrace risk and act to protect and restore the stability, integrity and beauty of the web of life.

Not bound by convention

Our success—and much of the fun—lies in developing new ways to do things."
https://www.patagonia.com/company-info.html

Kōnosuke Matsushita was a Japanese industrialist who founded Panasonic, the largest Japanese consumer electronics company. Matsushita's vision was *to "create material abundance by providing goods as plentifully and inexpensively as tap water. "This is how we can banish poverty, bring happiness to people's lives, and make this world a better place." Matsushita believed that "sole prosperity is not something that can be attained. True advancement and prosperity can only be achieved together with others."* https://tinyurl.com/th734d5

Matsushita focused on helping his employees to understand and believe in his principles. He insisted on celebrating talent and wanted employees to love their job. *"A man should not act only upon his own knowledge".* He insisted on collective wisdom, listening to everyone with a modest attitude to acquire knowledge and learn something.

Matsushita proposed a 250-year plan for the company, divided into 10 25-year periods that would be further divided into a 10-year construction phase, a 10-year active phase and a five-year fulfillment phase.

Set Your Vision

Step back and look at your corporate vision and philosophy: that which excites your employees, suppliers and customers to be part of your adventure. When younger, I enlisted into the US Army with the understanding that I might have to die for my country. Now, I am not asking people to die for their company, but we do want them to have a great sense of loyalty and support.

Sustaining profits and doing the right thing!

In the past with your sole commitment to make profits, gathered little loyalty from your employees. *"They should be happy that they have a job,"* is no longer sufficient.

Create a strong philosophy

As you will see, this commitment from the 181 CEO's is new and very important but missing is a clear philosophy to explain the purpose of the corporation. Kazuo Inamori started Kyocera in 1959 and today is one of the world's largest ceramic companies. He was asked by the Japanese government to become chairman of Japan Airlines when they went bankrupt on January 18, 2010.

"I really hated JAL. JAL was arrogant and didn't care about its customers." Kazuo Inamori, said. After two years the airline went from being bankrupt to making $2.5 billion in profits. It was truly a miracle. He focused on **"What is right to do as a human being!"** As he did at Kyocera, he expounded his philosophy to be committed to fair management and operation in compliance with the most fundamental human ethical and moral values and social norms.

He wanted the employees to be happy at work. He wanted them to give superior service to their customers. He wanted them to be properly compensated. He also wanted them to work very hard.

"Don't be greedy. Do not cheat people. Do not lie. Be honest. Do what is universally right as a human being and not what suits our own convenience."

Inamori delivered a philosophy of management and had it taught to every manager to teach to every employee. His formula for success: The Result of Life and Work =

Attitude x Effort x Ability. Do it. Evaluate yourself. On a scale of 1 to 100. For example, my attitude is 95 and my effort is 85 and my ability it 75 = 605,625. But a person who has 60X60X95 is only 342,000. That person has great ability but is not emotionally excited about their job or life. Inamori had everyone at JAL do this for their own evaluation.

Kazuo Inamori

JAL's philosophy:

- Base Criteria for Decision-Making on "Doing What Is Right as a Human Being."
- Have a Beautiful Mind
- Be Humble and Honest
- Always Be Cheerful and Positive
- A Small Good Is Like a Great Evil, while a Great Good May Appear Merciless
- Wrestle in the Center of the Ring
- Grasp Matters Simply
- Possess Opposing Extremes
- Accumulate Tedious Efforts with Passion
- Work Earnestly

42 **Sustaining profits and doing the right thing!**

- Accumulate Tedious Efforts
- Work with Voluntary Attention
- Fire Yourself Up
- Strive for Perfection
- Ability Will Improve
- Become a Wonderful JAL
- Each of Us Makes JAL
- Discuss Frankly
- Lead by Example
- Be the Center of the Vortex
- Valuable Lives Are Entrusted to Us in Our Work
- Be Thankful
- Put Yourself in the Customer's Position
- Have a Keen Sense of Profitability?
- Maximize Revenues and Minimize Expenses
- Elevate Our Cost-Consciousness
- Pursue Profit Fairly
- Manage the Company Based on Accurate Figures
- Unite Our Hearts
- Make the Best Baton Pass
- Align Mental Vectors
- "Work floor" Management
- Follow the Merit System
- Possess a Fighting Spirit
- Never Give Up Until We Succeed
- Boast and Make It Come True
- Possess True Courage
- Be Creative in Our Work
- Today Should Be Better Than Yesterday; Tomorrow Better Than Today.
- Conceive Optimistically, Plan Pessimistically, and Execute Optimistically

- Think Through to Visualize the Results
- Decide and Act with Speed
- Face Challenges with Courage
- Aim High

Kazuo Inamori, while at Kyocera, set up a unique Amoeba Management method. Amoeba Management divided the company into small units called "amoebas," with each amoeba leader being responsible for drafting plans and goals for the unit. In this system, every employee plays a major role and voluntarily participates in managing the unit, achieving what is known as "Management by All." The Amoeba Management System has been implemented at approximately 700 companies, including Kyocera, KDDI and Japan Airlines (JAL), where Inamori led the successful turnaround initiative.

Each amoeba is an independent profit-and-loss center directly linked to their respective markets, each amoeba manages its own profitability, allowing it to respond promptly to market changes.

1. Each amoeba pursues profit by practicing the principle of "Maximize revenues and minimize expenses;"

2. Each amoeba is an independent accounting unit that can buy and sell with other amoebas; and

3. Each amoeba makes monthly plans and records results using the Hourly Efficiency report, which is meant to be as easy to understand as a household budget.

4. Each amoeba is entrusted to a leader, who oversees business planning, management control, labor and purchasing. This system leads employees to develop managerial awareness.

5. All employees participate in managing the company by taking an active role in the operation of their

own amoebas. Employees take part in management by consolidating their skill sets and aligning their efforts toward shared goals. This builds a sense of purpose and achievement into the workplace.

To this end, every amoeba must:

1. Communicate its plan and goal in a vision that can be shared with all members;

2. Create a fiscal-year plan known as the "Master Plan," based on the strategies and goals of the entire company; and

3. Create monthly plans based on the Master Plan, and achieve the plan without fail.

The Twelve Management Principles use the question "What is the right thing to do as a human being?" as the most basic decision-making criteria. I believe that this universal philosophy transcends differences in nationality, ethnicity, culture and language.

Kazuo Inamori's The Twelve Management Principles

1.   Clearly State the Purpose and Mission of Your Business.
2.   Set Specific Goals.
3.   Keep a Passionate Desire in Your Heart.
4.   Strive Harder than Anyone Else.
5.   Maximize Revenues and Minimize Expenses.
6.   Pricing Is Management.
7.   Success Is Determined by Willpower.
8.   Possess a Fighting Spirit.
9.   Face Every Challenge with Courage.

10. Always Be Creative in Your Work.
11. Be Kind and Sincere.
12. Always Be Cheerful and Positive. Hold Great Dreams and Hopes in the Pureness of Your Heart.

Six Endeavors

1. Strive Harder than Anyone Else
2. Remain Humble
3. Reflect Daily
4. Appreciate Life
5. Do Good Deeds and Serve Others
6. Don't Dwell on the Past

What are the Seven Keys to Motivating Employees?

1. Embrace Employees as Partners
2. Gain the Respect and Admiration of Employees
3. Tell Employees About the Significance of Their Work
4. Have a Grand Vision for the Company
5. Clarify the Mission and Purpose of the Company
6. Continually Share Your Philosophy with Your Employees
7. Elevate Your Own Character

It is worth the time and effort to create your own philosophy to become more socially responsible, to create a great place where people can work happily, serve their customers well and also have the organization be very profitable.

Visual Consensus on Abstract Ideas (30 minutes)

Ask everyone to take two stickies (post-its), draw a house on one and draw what "social responsibility" means to you. (It's very important to make it a visual without the help of words.) Once everyone has gotten a chance to draw. Now, find another a person and gift your stickies to them. The person receiving should say, "thank you, this is nice"

Collect all the house sickies on an area of a whiteboard (or wall or a flipchart) and collect all the "social responsibility" stickies on another. Notice the similarities in the house drawings and the abundance of differences in the "social responsibility" one. Explain that the house falls in the category of "pictograph" and the other falls in the category of "ideograph." Pictographs are of tangible items and are easier to draw. Ideographs can be wicked to draw.

Look for patterns in the "social responsibility" stickies. Organize them by similarity. Ask participants to point to one they like that is not theirs and explain why. Use a voting mechanism (like dot voting on the stickies) to find which one is resonating.

Pick that one sticky as the center image of a new flipchart (or new space on the whiteboard or wall.) From here on, you can do a 5-Whys exercise or brainstorm on ideas to tackle it. Visual literacy is as important if not more for consensus building and rapidly connecting with each other.

Chapter IV - Delivering value to our customers

"We will further the tradition of American companies leading the way in meeting or exceeding customer expectations."

Do you treat customers the way you like to be treated?

This is an enormous challenge. While you state the above tradition of leading or exceeding customer expectations, in many cases the opposite has been true. Most large corporations have looked for ways to improve their own productivity instead of focusing on the customer's. Having the customer *"tangle"* with the automated phone answering systems or sending the calls to India or other low-cost countries does not show your sincerity. Missing in this is that the customer is King/Queen, someone to respect, cherish, and continually learn from.

When younger, we were all taught that the customer was King/Queen. Of course, it is obvious without customers, organizations do not survive. I remember the great customer service from the AT&T operators. All telephone calls were made through them and it was a joy to speak with them.

You were treated with respect at the local stores. And, I was taught to trust those that sold me their goods and services; maybe the only exception was the car salesman. I had personal contact with almost everyone that I bought things from: the candy store, the pharmacy, the butcher, the baker, the vegetable store, the tailor; each showed wonderful respect to their customers.

For me, the change began with the supermarket where the only contact you had was with the cashier who had very little product knowledge. Bigger businesses seemed to be more detached, less carrying as they were dependent on volume and not on the needs of each individual customer.

As the businesses grew bigger, the service was lessened. Many of them today operate as if they were monopolies.

When I was younger, companies took pride on how quickly they answered the telephone. And, I always had a person to speak with. Today, with these large companies almost always you get a computer to answer the telephone. I just laugh when the system says, *"We are recording this phone conversation for quality purposes."* Whose quality, surely not mine?

Unfortunately, artificial intelligence is being used to further the interests of the company, not yours. Not too long ago, I had trouble with my Internet service. I called Comcast, my provider. After a few rings a computer answered and asked for my needs. I told the computer, *"My router was not working properly."* A female recorded voice spoke and said she would reset my router and that I should wait ten minutes. I did and sure enough the router worked just fine. But, a day later it was down again.

I called Comcast back and got the same recording. It was quite frustrating for the computer would not let me speak to a representative. Finally, I hung up and called back, but this time I asked for sales help. Yes, if you call for sales, you will quickly get a human being, amazing. The salesperson told me to take the modem to a store. I did and they very quickly replaced my modem and an hour later sent me a request to evaluate the service given by the salesperson. However, they never asked me to evaluate the service given by the computer.

In 1980, I started a company called Productivity Inc. publishing a newsletter called Productivity.

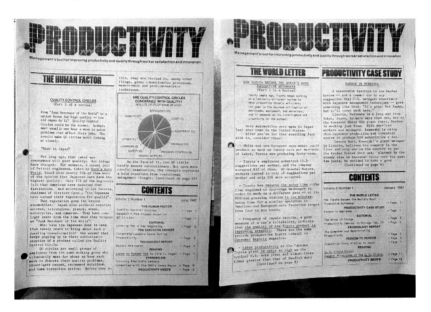

Magically, my timing was perfect as American productivity had recently declined, actually negative. My newsletter quickly grew to over 3000 subscribers. One day, I received a telephone call from Joe Synder. He said, *"Norman, I love your newsletter and I want to help you."* Joe was an independent consultant and one of his clients was the chairman of Chase Manhattan Bank. I said to Joe, *"I am going to run my first conference called Productivity the American Way at the Waldorf Astoria in New York City and I need*

keynote speakers: a CEO from a major corporation, a labor leader and a politician." I felt if I could get them, then I would be able to also attract industry speakers and also attract many attendees. Joe said, *"Give me a week."*

Joe did call back a week later and said, *"Norman, I got you Michael Rose, CEO of the Holiday Inns, the world's largest hotel chain, and Don Ephlin, senior vice-president of the UAW in charge of the Ford Motor Company account."* We also were able to get Stan Lundine, congressman from upstate New York and the conference was a great success. Joe never asked for anything in return.

Afterwards for the next ten years, I ran from two to ten conferences per year and was able to get a CEO from a top corporation to keynote every conference. Magically, back then I was able to reach their secretaries who were able to get them for me as keynote speakers. But today, it is virtually impossible for me to reach a top CEO. First, it is very difficult to find a phone number for the leaders of the top corporation and when I do, a *"guardian"* picks up the phone whose job is to make sure I cannot speak with them.

One speaker at a conference who worked for a large bank said, "My CEO once said, 'we could have such a great bank if we didn't have those lousy customers to deal with.'"

I am amazed that these CEOs shelter themselves from their customers. It is ironical, the customer keeps you alive! You can learn so much just from talking with them. The large corporations have thousands if not millions of customers and there is fear that the top managers will be inundated with calls from them, but that is not true. I have personally been able to speak with many famous people over the phone: Deming, Juran, Drucker, etc.

I recommend that every top executive spend at least one hour every day speaking with their customers - sure you might get some negative feedback, but that could be very helpful for you.

Taiichi Ohno, former VP at Toyota and creator of the Toyota Production System, would insist that the leader of his suppliers stand in a chalk circle in the middle of their factory for eight hours just to watch, observe, and look for waste. I recommend you do the same. Spend as much time learning both from your customers and employees. You will discover that *"gold,"* new opportunities, are lying there just waiting for you to recognize them.

Try to envision how you will improve customer service, treating customers as valuable contacts. **The trick is how you will improve your customer service without reducing your profits.**

Value adding is the way to profits; using customers as partners can serve you both. Your customer uses your product or service and can tell you how you to improve it. Ask the customer, what they do and do not like about your product or service. And teach your agents to always be on the side of the customer, **never to be defensive** - to feel that your company has to be protected. Get rid of the fear your agents carry - think of stopping the recording of phone calls. Once you fully trust an employee, you don't have to monitor them.

How to add value:

1.   **Look at the contact with the customer as a learning experience** for both the customer and your agent.

Sustaining profits and doing the right thing!
You can teach your customer wonderful things about your product or service and you surely can learn a lot from them.

2. **Ask the customer how you can improve your product or service.**

Paul Akers, president of Fastcap, a wood industry products company with around 50 employees, has added over 1000 new products from just listening to what the customer needed. The employees encourage the customers to come up with suggestions. (I talk about this, with Paul, later in the book.)

3. **Of course, your employees must get to know the products exceptionally well.**

One day in the past, I went to a Circuit City store with the intention of buying a new large TV set. I asked a salesman, *"Can you show me the best TV set?"* He pointed in the direction of the sets on the floor and walked away. I did the same. I walked out of the store.

A few weeks later, I was in Tokyo and went to a Bic Camera store (I wish we had those in America.) I asked a floor salesperson the same question. He took me over to a Sony TV and told me every great feature it had. He was filled with amazing knowledge and had great enthusiasm and I was overwhelmed. When I returned to America, I simply went to the Internet and searched for the same Sony set and ordered it. Ironically, a few days later, I broke my hip and was bed ridden for over a week - luckily however, I had the new Sony TV to watch all the football games over the holidays. And by the way, Circuit City decided they did not need trained salespeople and shortly, a little later, Circuit City went bankrupt.

I have been to Japan 93 times, as I published over 100 Japanese management books in English. From my past experiences, whenever I need help and call a Japanese company, I rarely need to speak to a specific person as the person who picks up the phone is filled with enormous knowledge about their company and the products or services. The employees spend a lot of time every day teaching each other. We should do the same.

I am so impressed with Bic Camera which has probably the world's largest variety of cameras, electronics, home appliances, personal computers, alcoholic beverages, golf equipment, bedding, drug store items, luxury brand products, bicycles, toys and *"you name it."* I was there a few weeks ago looking at their cameras; they carried probably every camera made anywhere in the world. It was just overwhelming.

I suggest you begin to relook at customer service as an opportunity to find new products and services; as an opportunity to learn with the customer; as an opportunity to fix existing problems and to continually refine your relationship with your customers. This requires a shift in attitude from only reducing costs to find ways to improve your relationship. You can do it surely. You can find ways to improve customer service and continue to make the profit you are looking for. In fact, as employees improve their knowledge of the company's products and services and have more knowledge of the customer's needs, sales will surely increase.

Today, many companies send their call centers to Asia: India, Philippines, Vietnam, South Africa, etc. There is nothing wrong in doing this but often the people there are not trained deeply enough and are not fully empowered to please and learn from those customers.

Empowerment is a key word: giving people the knowledge and power to serve the customer properly. To me it is nonsense that most people need their supervisor's help to make a decision. Trust your employees. Yes, they might make mistakes, but they will learn from those mistakes. And the mistakes made at their level will never be as costly as the mistakes made at the top - just look at the billions lost at Wells Fargo by their senior people. A teller is unable to lose a billion dollars.

Yes, improving customer service will initially cost more and when you increase your costs the profits decline, but as the customers have more knowledge, more appreciation about your products and services, higher profits will follow.

When I moved from the East Coast to Portland, Oregon, I had a problem with a flat tire. I went to the closest gasoline station but different from the East Coast, they did not repair tires. I was sent to a Les Schwab Tire Center. A mechanic quickly fixed the tire and surprisingly refused to accept any payment, not even a tip. I was amazed. It is now 20 years later, and I have always bought my tires from Les Schwab.

Treat us with respect and we can be customers for life. This is a win-win game. Believe it will happen. Improving your social responsibility does not require you to make sacrifices that will be detrimental to you.

Some suggestions to improve customer service:

We repeat **allow some of us to reach the CEO** or other members leading your organization. I guarantee you will not be inundated with calls. You are in business to serve your customers, but you cut off the opportunity for us to reach you. I recommend that every top person **spend at least one hour a day just talking to customers** and develop a mechanism that allows your company to really listen to the "voice of the customer." Don't be afraid of us. We are your customers.

In the last year, I have tried to reach senior people at top corporations. If I was lucky enough to get a phone number, I have not been able to get beyond the "guardian," who is there to prevent us from speaking to them.

Remove those guardians!

Tape the "guardians'" conversations and listen. I am sure you will be surprised how they treat your customers.

Kao Soap, one of the world's largest home products companies, relishes their hundreds of thousand customer's telephone calls. They have led to thousands of new products. Rethink the whole idea of customer service and see it as an asset not an unnecessary cost. Teach your employees how to fully respect the customer with the goal of keeping them for life. Even a customer complaint could lead to a new product, service or a new level of customer satisfaction. The challenge is for you to educate your customer service people and empower them more in speaking with your customers.

Reconsider the use of the telephone answering computer. As you increase your employee's knowledge, more of them answering the phone can directly serve the customer's needs.   Or Use AI more effectively. Allow artificial intelligence to enhance and enrich the interaction of your employees with your customers. Let the computer learn from each interaction to continuously improve the customer's experience. This needs a lot of work.

Do you still believe that the Customer is King/Queen? Do you treat the customer with the highest of respect? **Are you learning with the customer!**

I love to talk. I took a personality test recently and was amazed when it said that I need to listen more. It was right on target.

Look carefully at your customers and see how you can go back to the idea of how to serve them well. It is not easy to change. This new commitment to improve customer service is wonderful, but surely not easy to reverse a trend that has now existed for almost 50 years.

Be like Apple on their iPhone/computer side of the business which gives probably the best customer service in the world. I have an iPhone, an iPad, and I MacBook Pro and I constantly have needed support. I am just not a computer "geek." I call Apple to get support and am greeted by a computer telling me how good he is, good, but not really that great, however, I am able to quickly get someone to help me. I have called dozens of times and the people in support are great. They are patient and time is never an issue. They stay with me as long as necessary. Yes, you do pay a lot for the Apple products, but I have been very pleased.

Strangely, Apple on the App side of the business gives almost no service at all. I recently produced a Harada Method App which helps people pick and attain their goals. Once again, I needed help, but I have found over this past year to be impossible to find someone to speak with at Apple. I know that many, if not, most of the Apps are free to use. But I also know that the App side of the business is very profitable for Apple. It is a paradox, an enigma, for me to see Apple as the best and the worst in customer service. Hopefully, with this new commitment, Apple will figure out a way to give better service to their App developers.

Follow Hippocrates one of the world's first doctors.

Doctors traditionally take the Hippocratic Oath upon graduation from medical school.

"First, do no harm."

The Oath written by Hippocrates in 400 BC in Greece is still held sacred by physicians:

It is worth reading the modern version:

"I swear to fulfill, to the best of my ability and judgment, this covenant:

"I will respect the hard-won scientific gains of those physicians in whose steps I walk, and gladly share such knowledge as is mine with those who are to follow.

"I will apply, for the benefit of the sick, all measures that are required, avoiding those twin traps of overtreatment and therapeutic nihilism.

"I will remember that there is art to medicine as well as science, and that warmth, sympathy, and understanding may outweigh the surgeon's knife or the chemist's drug.

"I will not be ashamed to say, 'I know not,' nor will I fail to call in my colleagues when the skills of another are needed for a patient's recovery.

"I will respect the privacy of my patients, for their problems are not disclosed to me that the world may know. Most especially must I tread with care in matters of life and death. If it is given me to save a life, all thanks. But it may also be within my power to take a life; this awesome responsibility must be faced with great humbleness and awareness of my own frailty. Above all, I must not play at God.

"I will remember that I do not treat a fever chart, a cancerous growth, but a sick human being, whose illness may affect the person's family and economic stability. My responsibility includes these related problems, if I am to care adequately for the sick.

"I will prevent disease whenever I can, for prevention is preferable to cure.

"I will remember that I remain a member of society, with special obligations to all my fellow human beings, those sound of mind and body as well as the infirm.

"If I do not violate this oath, may I enjoy life and art, respected while I live and remembered with affection thereafter. May I always act so as to preserve the finest traditions of my calling and may I long experience the joy of healing those who seek my help."

I wish doctors would go back and read the oath and find ways to follow it.

Consider your own customer service oath?

Take the above from Hippocrates and write your own oath to your customers.

Mistake Proof your connection with your customers

One of my authors, Dr. Shigeo Shingo, a co-creator of the Toyota Production System (Lean) and I believe the world's best Industrial Engineer in the past 100 years, developed and perfected "poka-yoke," to virtually eliminate all defects in a manufacturing plant.

In America, we called it *"Fool Proofing."* In Japanese fool proofing is *"Baka Yoke."* Dr. Shingo one day in a factory said baka-yoke and a woman started to cry. Dr. Shingo asked her, *"Why are you crying?"* She said, *"I am not a fool."* Dr. Shingo immediately changed the word to poka-yoke, mis-proofing.

I have been to a factory where I saw thousands of very simple devices, sensors, to prevent mistakes from happening. I am sure we can do the same in America to improve customer service.

Encourage people to reveal all of their mistakes, to share them and learn from them

In school, when you made a mistake your grade went down. All of us were taught to not make mistakes, but ironically, we learn the most from our mistakes. At work people are filled with fear about making mistakes and hide them for they are often punished when they make a mistake.

One day, leading a study mission in Japan, I visited Hino Motors, manufacturing trucks and buses. On the factory floor, I saw a large chart board   with many sheets of paper, each with a picture of a worker and many words were written. Also, there was a sticker with either a smiley face or a sad face.

A mistake board

I asked a manager to please explain the chart. He said, *"That is a mistake board and whenever a worker makes a mistake, they go over to the board to write it down. The smiley face means the worker knew how to not repeat the mistake while the sad face meant the worker needs help to learn how not to repeat it."*

This mistake board could have a very powerful effect on changing your culture. Try it. Imagine everyone is revealing their mistakes so as not to repeat them. It is a wonderful way to take "fear" out of the workplace.

Create a no blame culture

Sustaining profits and doing the right thing!

When you make a mistake, you might regret it, but hopefully you learned something and then quickly forgave yourself. But curiously when someone else makes a mistake often they are punished and most of them live in fear. Change this now and look at all mistakes as opportunities to learn and grow.

7. Make all of your products safe for your customers.

Profit have driven many of the world's ills. When profit is the only major concern of a CEO, many shortcuts are taken. I will only cover a few, but we hope you will carefully look at your products and services and see how you can become like the doctor and "do no harm."

At 15, like all of my friends I started to smoke. My elder brother smoked, my parents did not. Eventually, when later at work, I was smoking three packs a day. I only really liked to smoke a few a day, but I was "hooked." I was addicted and since it was socially accepted, I just did like it like others did. Luckily, blessed, at age 37 I was able to do a *"cold turkey"* and give it up entirely. However, it actually took around 15 years to fully give up the desire to smoke.

Unfortunately, almost all of us are addicted to habits. Some are helpful but many are harmful. Question? For a corporation to be socially responsible is it obligated to help people break their addictions? With profit solely as a corporate objective, in the past, many corporations just took advantage of these addictions. Like in the movie with Peter Sellers, Dr. Strangelove, from Tom Lehrer's lyrics, *"Vonce der rockets are up / Who cares vhere dey come down / That's not my department / Says Wernher von Braun."*

Now, with a new commitment to become socially responsible to our customers, can you and will you totally re-examine the effects your products have on people and the environment? It will not be easy, but we do need the CEO's to rise to the equation, *"Somebody has to save the world."*

We hope to give you in this book the concepts and tools that you may want to apply to transform   your business and your life and to create more value for your customers, for society and for yourself.

In America, around 40% of adults are obese. I am sure that most know why they are overweight and also know the detrimental effects, to their health, of being heavy. We know that "sugar," especially high fructose corn syrup and products coming from grains: wheat, rice, pasta, etc. are the major cause, but we are addicted to our habits. Can we somehow teach moderation? Can we still advertise and produce our products producing a minimum amount of damage? I know you can.

I am sure you know the story about Purdue Pharma and the wonderful drug, OxyContin, discovered to ease the pain of many people. My first wife suffered tremendously from migraines. Once a month she went to bed and lived like a vegetable waiting for the hours to pass to take another pill. Yes, the drug effectively made her life a little bit more livable, and miraculously she did not become addicted like so many other people did to OxyContin. Maybe, there was a way to administer the drug properly to help people in their pain and to help them also not become addicted. But greed overpowered Purdue and they followed the words of Milton Friedman literally. I am sure Milton Friedman expected the corporate world to pursue profits without administering harm to our society. (70,000 people die each year in America from drugs.)

I know that pressure from your stockholders can be harsh. I know the pressure on you to deliver you quarterly profits can be unbelievable. You can easily lose your job and the wonderous material life you have, but this new commitment is very important to the rest of us. I am sure you will rise to this new challenge and continue to be successful.

Can you stop recording for quality purposes?

Be sincere! Why are you really recording your employees? Are your calls recorded for quality purposes? It is annoying for the customer to always have to listen to this statement. You don't give us a choice to not record. I know you want to protect yourself from liability suits, but do you record all your messages for quality purposes? Maybe you can record new employees until they are fully trained.

Teach and trust all of your employees. Ask them to help each other to sustain your high level of quality.

Of course, quality is vitally important in both customer service and in your products. The focus on quality helped Japan go from an undeveloped country to a world class competitor. I often go to Japan and constantly admire their quality service and products. For example, I love strawberries. I often time my trips to Japan in March so that we can both see the cherry blossoms (my wife is Japanese) and also pick those delicious strawberries. Now why in America do we buy wonderful looking strawberries that taste like straw?

9.   Offer more phone numbers to reach specific departments

This can reduce the annoying robotic answering computer. You want your interactions to serve the customer's needs. Of course, you want to improve your productivity but also consider the customer's productivity. Just do the right thing!

10.   Use the voice of the customer to improve your product and services

Many companies take lots of surveys but then ignore them. Who has the time to read them all? Listen to the customer and ask them for their recommendations to improve your customer service.

Teach your employees to have dialogs with their customers to learn from them and to create a real relationship. You can train people to become loyal customers. Watch football on TV on Saturday or Sunday and see the millions of fans that attend the games. Why? Most have developed a loyalty with their favorite team. You can do the same.

11.　　Talk to us – stop sending to Internet or chat

Chat can be good, but it is much better to talk and learn with the customer directly. Set up your internal mechanisms that contacts with customers is a positive experience, an opportunity to learn from the customer and also to improve your products or services.

The 181 CEO's represent the biggest companies in America, but they should imagine that can operate as if they were small giving more and more autonomy, mastery and purpose to all of their employees. I recommend you all study the work of Kazuo Inamori, probably the best manager in Japan, who developed when at Kyocera the Amoeba management system. He divided up this large company into very small amoebas, small departments, and gave power to the small group to run their department as if it was their own company with their own P&L statement. Kyocera a 16-billion-dollar company has never lost any money in any year in the last 50 years.

12.　　Define and teach value to your customers

When I was younger, my parents never had any antiques. In fact, I had the original Superman and Spiderman comics, but my mother threw them away, only worth today around one million each. The neighbors had antiques, but my mother called them junk.

Yes, you can drink tea from a paper cup or from a beautiful ceramic one.

What is the difference? The taste is similar, but the ceramic cup has a real value that you can see, feel, and touch. As you drink your tea, the experience is so much better. And people are willing to pay more when you add value to your product which adds real value to their lives.

What is so unique about a painting by Van Gogh or Rembrandt? Why do we pay millions for them? One reason could be originality, but I know that there is real value that comes from the *"living"* energy from the master that created the piece. Just looking at a great piece of art somehow adds real enjoyment and value to your life.

Sustaining profits and doing the right thing!

Night Watch by Rembrandt

One day a year ago, I was in Kyoto and we stopped at an Incense shop. I like to burn incense when I meditate each morning. I noticed an incense burner selling for around $20,000. I asked the clerk if the burner was an antique. He said, *"no, it was new."* I was amazed that the new incense burner was selling for $20,000, but it was probably made by one of Japan's Living Masters.

I have been to 52 different countries in my life, 93 times to Japan, 75 times to the Caribbean, numerous times to India and Europe, etc. I love to travel and learn from other cultures, always with the idea, can I bring back something that we can learn from? Recently, I visited Finland, Netherlands and Japan.

In Finland, I lectured at Aalto University and I had fun with the students but frankly as part of my teaching, I could not get them to pick a new goal; they were just too happy the way things were in their country: everyone can get a free college education, the young students have a choice to either go to college or to learn a trade, they are fully protected medically, and they live in a beautiful environment.

Amsterdam was also fun walking along the canals and passing so many little shops and restaurants. I passed one store where people were lined up to buy cookies. I asked those on the line if they tasted the cookies. *"No,"* they said, *"But the cookies must be great if people are always standing in a line to get them."* Of course, I also had to stand in the line to taste - and they were very good.

13.   Quality is always number one

I have published over 250 management books, over 100 are translations from Japan. From these books we discovered the Toyota Production System (Lean) and Total Quality Management (TQM).

In 1950, W. Edwards Deming was brought to Japan at the behest of General Douglas MacArthur, who grew frustrated at being unable to complete so much as a phone call without the line going dead due to Japan's shattered postwar economy. While in Japan, Dr. Deming was invited to

Sustaining profits and doing the right thing!
lecture to members of the <u>Japanese Union of Scientists and Engineers</u> (JUSE). Before speaking, members of JUSE told Dr. Deming that they would get 350 engineers to hear his lectures. Dr. Deming said, *"No, I want to speak to 350 CEOs."* Miraculously, they got 350 CEOs to hear him. They asked him, *"How can we catch up to America?"* Deming's message to Japan's chief executives was that improving <u>quality</u> would reduce expenses, while increasing <u>productivity</u> getting them market share and allow them to catch America.

*"However, no matter how excellent your technicians, you who are leaders, must strive for advances in the improvement of product quality and uniformity if your technicians are to be able to make improvements. **The first step, therefore, belongs with management.** First, your company technicians and your factories must know that you have a fervor for advancing product quality and uniformity and a sense of responsibility for product quality."*

A number of Japanese manufacturers applied his techniques widely and experienced heretofore unheard-of levels of quality and productivity. The improved quality combined with the lowered cost created new international demand for Japanese products.

In was June 24, 1980, one month after starting my Productivity newsletter when I saw "*If Japan can ... Why can't we?* It was an <u>American</u> <u>television</u> <u>episode</u> broadcast by <u>NBC News</u> as part of the <u>television show</u> *"NBC White Paper"* and it introduced me to <u>W. Edwards Deming</u> and Joseph Juran.

The report details how the **Japanese** captured the world automotive and electronics markets by following

Deming's advice to practice continual improvement and think of manufacturing as a system, not as bits or pieces.

During the 1980s, Japan was seen to be a manufacturing powerhouse while American industry was struggling to keep pace. It was strongly believed that Japanese manufacturing techniques were uniquely developed for and suited to the Japanese culture, and thus unsuited for American culture. It was wrong! It was a myth!

Dr Deming said, *"The Japanese realized that the gains that you get by statistical methods are gains that you get without new machinery, without new people. Anybody can produce quality if he lowers his production rate. That is not what I am talking about. Statistical thinking and statistical methods are to Japanese production workers, foremen, and all the way through the company, a second language. In statistical control you have a reproducible product hour after hour, day after day. And see how comforting that is to management: they now know what they can produce, they know what their costs are going to be.*

I think that people here expect miracles. American management thinks that they can just copy from Japan—but they don't know what to copy!

I ask people in management what proportion of this problem arises from your production worker. And the answer is always: All of it! That's absolutely wrong.

There's nobody that comes out of a School of Business that knows what management is, or what its deficiencies are. There's no one coming out of a School of Business that ever heard of the answers that I'm giving your questions—or probably even thought of the questions."

After watching the TV program, I called both Dr. Deming and Dr. Juran. A few weeks later, I visited Dr. Juran in his office and interviewed him for my newsletter. He was absolutely brilliant and one of the best speakers I had ever heard. I highly recommend you get his videos and learn quality from the great master.

Subsequently, I flew to Atlanta to hear and meet Dr. Deming and I met with him and made a terrible mistake. I said to Dr. Deming, *"I want to publish your books."* He said, *"I don't write books."* Foolishly, I didn't just record his workshop and write and publish his book. Many years later, Mary Walton attended his workshop and wrote the best-selling book, **The Deming Management Method.**

Worthy of your attention is to read, study and apply Dr. Deming's 14 key principles for management for transforming business effectiveness. It can be the heart of your new socially responsible system.

Deming's 14 points:

1. Create constancy of purpose toward improvement of product and service, with the aim to become competitive and stay in business, and to provide jobs.
2. Adopt the new philosophy. Western management must awaken to the challenge, learn their responsibilities and take on leadership for change.
3. Cease dependence on inspection to achieve quality. Building quality into the product in the first place.
4. End the practice of awarding business on the basis of price tag alone. Move toward a single supplier for any one item, and on a long-term relationship of loyalty and trust.
5. Improve constantly and forever the system of production and service. Improve quality and productivity, and thus constantly decrease cost.
6. Institute training on the job. Give all your employees the opportunity to grow.

7. Institute leadership — the aim of leadership is to help people and machines to do a better job. Management and supervision must improve.
8. Drive out fear. Make the workplace where everyone may work effectively for the company.
9. Break down barriers between staff areas. Have everyone work as a team to foresee problems of production.
10. Eliminate slogans, exhortations and targets for the work force. Ask for zero defects and new levels of productivity. The bulk of the causes of low quality and low productivity belong to the system and thus lie beyond the power of the work force.
11. Eliminate numerical quotas. Substitute leadership.
12. Remove barriers to pride of workmanship. The responsibility of supervisors must be changed from sheer numbers to quality.
13. Institute a vigorous program of education and self-improvement.
14. Take action to accomplish the transformation.

Dr. Deming

I was a student at New York University Graduate School of Business, and I told a friend, Howard, that I was going to take a statistics class in the next term. Howard said, *"Don't take statistics. It is much too hard."* I foolishly listened to Howard. Dr. Deming was the teacher. I could have met him 30 years earlier than I did if I just listened to my own heart and not to someone else. In fact, my biggest problem in life was not always listening to Jimny Cricket. (My own conscious.)

15.   Run lots of contests with your employees focused on improving customer service

My favorite hotel in Tokyo is the Imperial and as a member when I check in, they don't need to look at my passport or see my credit card and they will automatically upgrade me to a better room. They always give superior service. Go there just to watch and study what they do.

I love breakfast on the 17th floor where the eggs and Danish are superb. On one visit with my study group, I asked the Maître d'hotel to please let me meet the chef who baked the Danish. I met him and asked, *"What do you do to get such great pastry?"* He said, *"Every month we have a contest with the 25 chefs at our hotel to improve our food. They cook and taste and pick the best.*

Also, I entered the national pastry contest in Tokyo, and I won. They then sent me to Paris for the international conference which I also won."

I have one talent which is to find the great talent in the world. From meeting them, when I owned Productivity Press, I published those 250 books.

You will see all over Japan these contests to support their quest for quality. They even have an annual contest to recognize the best cleaning service. Haneda airport in Tokyo has been recognized five years in a row to be the cleanest airport in the world. The highest award was given to Niitsu, a

Sustaining profits and doing the right thing!
cleaning lady that worked at Haneda airport in Tokyo. She was nominated as the best cleaning lady in all of Japan. She cleans toilets. She was on national television.

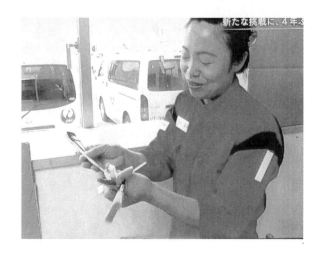

Japan also recognizes their master craftspeople. The Japanese government, with the goal of preserving important intangible cultural assets, provides a special annual grant of 20,000 dollars (2 million yen) to Living National Treasures. Currently 59 individuals in Japan are awarded the title of Living National Treasure with 7 categories: pottery, textiles, lacquerware, metalworking, dollmaking, woodworking and papermaking.

Last year, I visited a ceramic artist and was especially attracted to a large plate with a painted drawing. It was a fine piece of art, but it had a price of around $2,200 and it was new. I asked and was told that the artist was a national treasure.

High skill is appreciated in Japan and people are willing to pay for it. I feel this is true in most aspects in life. If you just continue to grow, you will improve your value and should have a marvelous life.

Unfortunately, in America, you can go through 13 years of grammar school and graduate with no skill to make a living. The lucky ones can go on to college, but a vast number go out into the workplace and get boring and repetitive jobs. We should be taught how to cook, how to design and make clothes, how to become a carpenter, electrician, plumber, tinsmith, computer programmer, etc.

Toyota recently also started a mastery program where they designate the high skilled people as "masters," someone that people can look up, to learn from and hopefully some day they will also become a master.

Imagine having contests in your company to recognize your greatest talents. It is easy to do, and the reward can be a just a simple medal or certificate.

Unfortunately, our educational system is very poor in teaching us value, but you can do this to expand your market, to enrich the lives of your customers and recognize your employee's exceptional efforts.

I recommend you consider running contests throughout your organization to support your new concept of being socially responsible. Get everyone on the "band wagon."

14.   Make safe responsible products

Stuck in my mind is a saying from the movie The Graduate, *"I want to say just one word to you, plastics. There is a great future in plastics."* And he was right. Plastics was so successful, but it was also indestructible and now covers the earth, especially our oceans.

The proliferation of plastic products in the last several decades has been extraordinary. Quite simply, humans are addicted to this nearly indestructible material. We are producing over 300 million tons of plastic every year, 50% of which is for single-use purposes – utilized for just a few moments, but on the planet for at least several hundred years.

One in three species of marine mammals have been found entangled in marine litter and 90% of all sea birds have plastic pieces in their stomach.

Many marine organisms can't distinguish common plastic items from food. Animals who eat plastic often starve because they can't digest the plastic and it fills their stomachs, preventing them from eating real food.

There are currently 5 trillion pieces of plastic waste in the world's oceans, according to The Ocean Cleanup, a project dedicated to ridding the ocean of waste.

More than 800 species of marine animals are affected by plastics, and the entire marine ecosystem is now contaminated.

Yes, there was a great future in plastics, too good and now the earth and sea are threatened. Who will address this problem? It is a challenge, but industry has to rise to the occasion. Hopefully you will find a way to stop the production of indestructible plastics. Recently, in Vancouver, Washington, we are required to put our eatable garbage into biodegradable bags before disposing them. And New York City just announced the elimination of the single use plastic bag.

To be socially responsible, you must look more at making only safe products. Socially responsibility is a challenge. I know you can do it!

15.   Reduce harmful ingredients

Monsanto's roles in agricultural changes, biotechnology products, lobbying of government agencies, and roots as a chemical company, resulted in controversies. The company once manufactured controversial products such as the insecticide DDT, PCBs, Agent Orange, and recombinant bovine growth hormone. Its seed patenting model was criticized as biopiracy and a threat to biodiversity as invasive species. Bayer bought Monsanto and because of the product Roundup - over 4,000 cancer patients are suing Monsanto in numerous state courts for failure to warn the public about the risk of cancer associated with their glyphosate-based weed killer.

80 **Sustaining profits and doing the right thing!**

Monsanto was at times financially very successful but Bayer plans to drop the name. Monsanto seeds have been resistant to weeds and insects and has added to the food supply in the world, but the negative side effects have been ignored and in the long term can have disastrous effects to our food supply and the environment. And with the growth of organic foods those seeds might eventually disappear.

Both short-term versus long-term effects have to be studied carefully. I liked the philosophy of Konosuke Matsushita who started Panasonic (Panasonic has 271,869 employees, around 580 subsidiary companies, 80 billion in sales). He wrote a 250-year plan to support his long-term vision.

"He who gains time gains everything." --Benjamin Disraeli

In 1932, Konosuke Matsushita, the founder of the Panasonic corporation, gathered his 1200 employees and announced a 250-year plan for his company. Panasonic had already been in business since 1918, and Matsushita himself was already 38 years old.

Matsushita's 250-year plan might strike some people as absurd, but it helped orient his company toward a visionary mission for itself.

"Long-term thinking is an extraordinary lever that lets people accomplish things they couldn't do otherwise." --Jeff Bezos

In his book on Matsushita's management style, John Kotter notes "*that setbacks are not necessarily career-killers, that they can in fact nurture big, idealistic goals and continuous growth, and that in a changing environment,* **lifelong learning is the quality most responsible for great success** *or unusual achievements."*

16.   Respond quickly

Around 1955, Toyota was running out of cash and could not borrow from the bank. Faced with this problem Taiichi Ohno, VP of Production at Toyota, looked at the factory floor with the mountains of inventory and realized that if he could reduce the inventory, Toyota would have all the cash they needed.

Taiichi Ohno

Ohno asked Shigeo Shingo, independent consultant, to reduce the change over time at a punch press from four hours to two. Shingo said, *"Okay"* and he sat and watched the changeovers. A few days later, Ohno came over to Shingo and said, *"Two hours is no good. We need to be able to do it in less than 10 minutes."* Shingo said again, "okay" and continued to study. Miraculously, Shingo was able to reduce the change-over times to less than 10 minutes. Long change-over times required the production of the mountains of inventory.

In November 1980, prior to going to Japan on my first study mission, I visited an Oldsmobile plant in Tarrytown, New York. They were manufacturing 1000 cars a day with two shifts. In the factory floor was a 1000 of everything needed to assembly the cars and just outside the plant were railroad trains with a least another three days of inventory. (I also noticed employees on the line working very slowly, doing deadly boring work. I asked the guide about this and he said, *"We have a man in the plant whose only job for 43 years was to put tires on the line."*)

When I visited Toyota in February of 1981, I saw only 20 engines on the floor, and I noticed the workers moving at least three times faster than at Oldsmobile.

Ohno had discovered the value of responding quickly and created the concept of Just-in-time which gave Toyota a tremendous advantage over American automobile producers.

I want to mention also the "power," that Ohno used to transform Toyota from a producer of "cheap and junky cars," to become one of the largest most successful companies in the world.

One: Ohno was almost always on the factory floor watching, observing, and making suggestions on improvement. He would draw a circle with chalk on the factory floor and demand that Toyota supplier's top managers stand in the circle all day and just watch and look for waste. Ohno knew the power of observation and observing where the product was being made.

"I told everyone that they weren't earning their pay if they left the standardized work unchanged for a whole month. The idea was to let people know that they were responsible for making continual improvements in the work procedures and for incorporating those improvements in the standardized work."

Muda - wastes
Muri - overburden
Mura - unevenness

Two: **Ohno would constantly demand the "impossible" from people.**

DEMAND THE IMPOSSIBLE

He would walk over to a department with 10 people and tell the manager to run it with seven and give them three months to do it. **He would not tell them how to do it. He just challenged them.** He had no idea if they could do it or not, but he also knew that if he didn't ask, they would hardly ever change to that degree. One day at Toyota Gosei, a top supplier to Toyota, Ohno in front of a building, turned to the president of the company and said, *"At Toyota we do not have warehouses. I want you to turn this building into a machine shop and retrain everybody there to become a mechanic. I give you one year to do it."* He then just walked away.

"I told everyone that they weren't earning their pay if they left the standardized work unchanged for a whole month. The idea was to let people know that they were responsible for making continual improvements in the work procedures and for incorporating those improvements in the standardized work." - Taiichi Ohno

I had a lot to do with bringing Lean to America as I was Ohno's and Shingo's publisher. Millions of companies and hospitals are attempting to follow Toyota and become lean but very few do. (According to a survey by John Ballis of 10,000 people surveyed only 1.6% say they are doing Lean after 10 years.) Why? I feel because the leaders of Lean do not exercise the power of Ohno.

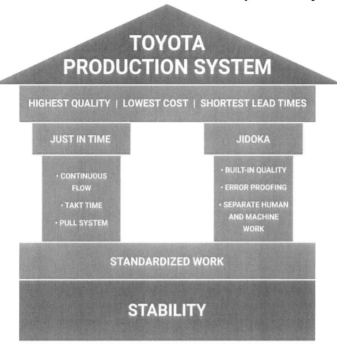

Ohno focused on 7 wastes, non-value adding activity, to be eliminated:

1. Inventory
2. Transportation
3. Motion
4. Defects
5. Waiting
6. Overproduction
7. Over-processing

I added one:

8. Underutilization of people's talents

Eliminating these wastes is wonderful for they do not add value to your products. Also producing products that do not sell and that nobody wants – that is a major waste to society and seems to me even more important than the standard wastes.

If you are in manufacturing, you should also be pursuing the elimination of these wastes, but foolishly, many people in non-manufacturing are also pursing the same wastes. Hospitals for example are using these wastes in their Lean efforts, but those are not their prime problems. Hospitals major problems are: hundreds of thousands of people are dying from medical error, 50% of our doctors are going through "burnout," medical costs in America far exceed any other developed country and the quality of our care does not rank close to many of them, and the total system needs adjusting: doctors for example have to make all the decisions on patient care.

Lean is great, but you should determine what your specific problems, wastes, are and then go after eliminating them relentlessly. Copying others could be great but as Rudi once said, *"If you are digging for oil, you should be sure that there is oil underground where you are digging."*

Ohno is also known for his "Ten Precepts" to think and act to win. First say, *"I can do it."* And try before everything. You might like these:

1. You are a cost. First reduce waste.
2. First say, "I can do it." And try before everything.
3. The workplace is a teacher. You can find answers only in the workplace.
4. Do anything immediately. Starting something

right now is the only way to win.

     5. Once you start something, persevere with it. Do not give up until you finish it.

     6. Explain difficult things in an easy-to-understand manner. Repeat things that are easy to understand.

     7. Waste is hidden. Do not hide it. Make problems visible.

     8. Valueless motions are equal to shortening one's life.

     9. Re-improve what was improved for further improvement.

     10. Wisdom is given equally to everybody. The point is whether one can exercise it.

17.   Delegate "power!"

Jack Katzen was a senior VP of AVCO, a two-billion-dollar company, who called me and asked me to teach him what this new quality movement was all about. *"We have quality problems and I need help."* As an example, AVCO Lycoming was a sole source supplier of M1 tank engines that were failing in Europe exercises and AVCO felt threatened of losing their sole source contract.

Of course, I agreed to help. AVCO at the time owned around 10 corporations. Jack and I flew to each of the corporations and met with the presidents and their senior staff. Jack said to them, *"Don (the CEO of AVCO) wants you to write a quality plan for your corporation and submit it back to us in 30 days."* **Jack took the power of the president.**

When we received all 10 plans, Jack replicated them and sent them all 10 back to the presidents and told them to study what their peers had written and re-write their annual plan again. They studied all the plans and re-submitted their own plan.

Four years later, Jack was the Assistant Secretary of Defense and invited me to the Pentagon. He took me into a room filled with Generals and Admirals (earlier in my life I was in the US Army, but I never saw a General before.) Jack said to the group, ***"I want you to meet the man that saved my company AVCO $400,000,000."*** I am sorry that I didn't have that recorded.

Jack, amazingly, inspired the presidents to share their knowledge and lead the transformation of AVCO. Your challenge is how can you really empower people in your organization to support your new endeavor to become *"socially responsible."* Not easy, but you will do it!

I was with a VP from a company with over 1000 employees and he said, *"I wish my president would lead the new Lean efforts."* The VP felt he did not have the power to do it. Many senior people do not realize that they can take the power of the CEO to get things done. Test it. Start to share this story with others and see if they can take the power to delegate effectively. The CEO has to trust others and allow this to happen. Empowering others does not mean you will lose your power, not at all. Empowering others can make your organization much more effective.

But this is true at every level. Learn how to share power.

18. Listen and learn together with your customer

I do love to teach, to present. I have keynoted many conferences and have run many workshops, but honestly it was very difficult for me to listen. I was the president of Productivity Inc. – Press and fortunately the company was very successful. The success went to my head and I made almost of the decisions. People would come to me with a problem or a suggestion and truly, I rarely asked them for their advice. I just told them what to do.

This probably came from my education for as a child the teacher would *"teach"*, and rarely ever would they ask for my advice or learn with me. Of course, they would ask questions to test me but never to create a learning dialog that brings out the best from both of us. Yes, the teaching experience is where both the teacher and the student are learning from each other.

This is true with your customers. There should be real dialog between you both. It is easy for me to *"sell,"* but not too easy for me to learn. I come to a meeting with a *"prepared agenda,"* to sell what I have, not to find out first what the customer really needs.

I received a phone call from James Bramson, president of Spraying Systems, the world's largest producer of specialty nozzles. He wanted to meet with Jim Swartz one of my authors. I called Jim and we both went to Chicago to meet with James. At the meeting with James, his treasurer and VP of Sales, Jim asked, *"What are your strategic problems?"* James said, *"We have a 70% world share on nozzles, but our competition is producing higher quality nozzles and they can produce new nozzles much faster than us."* Jim immediately said, *"I can definitely help solve your problems, but frankly I just don't have the time to work with you."*

To me this was brilliant. First, Jim did not try to sell James on his expertise and secondly, how do you tell a president of a 250 million-dollar company that you have no time for him? Of course, Jim consulted with Spraying Systems, actually for the next 20 years; taught them Lean; solved their problems and helped them grow the company.

19.   Take advantage of negative feedback

I know that criticism is hard to digest, but if you can take it in like *"fuel,"* look at it like a *"jewel,"* amazing opportunities can be found. Focusing on customer needs, criticism, and complaints can help you find new products and services.

Since people are caught in their habits, most sitting with fear, you should role play how to handle negative feedback. And try to teach people not to become defensive when the customer complains. Remember the golden rule: ***"The customer is always right,"*** even when they are wrong. And try to never punish people when they make a mistake doing something that serves the customer.

Wells Fargo, mentioned earlier, like most banks, sets up *"Rules"* for their employees to follow. They are fearful that the tellers will lose money, but the reality is that the teller can lose very little money while the CEO can lose the company billions. Wells Fargo collected millions of dollars in fees and interest to which the bank was not entitled, harmed the credit ratings of certain customers, and unlawfully misused customers' sensitive personal information, according to the Justice Department, which announced on Feb. 21, 2020 that the banking company has agreed to pay an additional $3 billion to settle the charges.

If a teller, made a mistake costing a few dollars, they could be fired with very little compensation, but when the CEO left the bank, he received $130 million. Doesn't really sound fair.

A few years ago, I tried to call the CEO at Wells Fargo and got a "guardian." He would not let me speak with the CEO or any officer or any of their assistants. I was sorry, for I thought I had some good ideas to share with them. I believe it is always good to get some outside perspective and it would have only taken a. few moments to listen to me.

Today, March 16, 2020, Wells Fargo's board canceled the $15 million stock bonus it gave to former CEO Tim Sloan last year. Sloan also received no severance from the company when he resigned in March 2019.

One day a woman at a Uniqlo store in Tokyo was carrying a baby and asked the manager if she could call a doctor for her child. The manager said, *"I am sorry,   but we have a rule that we cannot let the customer use our phones."* The woman   left and went next door and was able to find a phone to call an ambulance.

Subsequently, she wrote a letter to Mr. Tadashi Yanai, the president of Uniqlo and actually the richest person in Japan. He read the letter and immediately   contacted Takashi Harada and said, *"I need your help.   I want my employees to follow the rules but also, they need to know when they can change them for the benefit of the customer. Please come and help us."* (I will write about the Harada Method later in the book.)

20.   Taste it!

Many years ago, I was invited to have lunch at the Colgate Club in New York City by an executive of the Advertising Council. Towards the end of the lunch, he asked me what I would like for dessert. I said, *"Melon, but most times I am very disappointed in receiving hard melon."* He said, *"Norman, I also like melon and you will not be disappointed here. Here the melons are always great."* How? He said, *"I once asked the chef how he always served great melons."* He said, *"Easily, before we serve the customer, we cut open the melon and we taste it."*

Funny, but a few weeks later I was at lunch at another restaurant and asked the waitress to get me a great piece of melon. She said, *"How will I know if the melon is great."* I said, *"Open it and taste it."* She said, *"But what do I do with it if it is bad?"* (*"Of course, if it is bad give it to the customer!"*)

I don't know about you but most often I am served hard melons at restaurants. Waiters and waitresses are just not allowed to taste the food. And yet, it is so simple. Just ask your employees to always give great customer service and offer only the finest products possible and allow them to do it. Just, *"take off the cuffs."*

21. Customer service is promptness, politeness, professionalism and personalization.

Now this is a real challenge. In the past, customer service has been viewed as an expense and large corporations have shifted most of this to Asia and other low-cost countries around the world. But now you have a new commitment to become socially responsible and to now focus on providing your customers with new levels of superior service. You do have choices; one is to bring it all back-home to call centers in America and another is to really take it more seriously and get out there and give those people overseas the training they need to give superior service. It is not easy, for they come from another culture with their own values. I feel that most of the foreign call centers are owned by sub-contractors, not real employees working for you. If this is true, then how can you work with your suppliers as if they were part of your company. (We will address this issue more closely when we write about improving your supplier relations.)

Your challenge is how to improve this service without adding to your costs.

India and the other low-cost countries are enticing, and hopefully it can work for you when you change your concept of the relationship.

A year ago, I was involved with Toyota Tsusho. We were going to invest in creating a Harada Method APP together, but they determined that the new APP would cost over $350,000. They decided not to do it. One of their employees left the company and asked me to help do it. I foolishly went and searched the Internet and found an APP provider in India that was willing to build the APP both in IOS and Android for only $30,000. I say foolishly for we signed a contract whereby they agreed to produce the IOS version in three months - it actually took them a year to do. I got caught and the Android never really was completed. (Sometimes when you buy "cheap" you get "cheap.")

Set up an exact process with your suppliers that will get you promptness, politeness, professionalism and personalization. Write out the entire scenario and set up the necessary tests, procedures and constraints necessary.

22.   Customer service is the process of helping people find what they want during the entire transaction cycle

Of course, if the product is high priced then you feel that you can spend the time to stay with the customer until the customer is fully satisfied, but what do you do when the product is not high priced:

#1: Empathy
#2: Deep Product Knowledge = Confidence
#3: Active Listening
#4: Go the Extra Mile
#5: Patience
#6: Handle the Curveballs
#7: Clarity
#8: Always Follow Up
#9: Don't be afraid to outsource
#10: Build Trust Through Transparency
#11: Use Positive Statements
#12: Stay Calm
#13: Use Active Voice
#14: Anticipate (and Handle) Objections
#15: Closing skills
#16: Always Be Learning
https://www.jitbit.com/news/customer-service-skills/

23.   Customer service is the degree to which a product fails to meet, meets or exceeds customer's expectations. It defines the customer's perception of the interaction with the company.

We have a very good friend in Japan Noriaki Kano famous for inventing the Kano Quality Model. The Kano Model is an insightful way of understanding, categorizing, and prioritizing 5 types of Customer Requirements (or potential Features) for new products and services.

1. Attractive (producing unexpected value)
2. One-Dimensional (defined by their magnitude – essentially the more, the better)
3. Must-Be (those preferences described as "need to haves")
4. Indifferent (essentially a lack of a preference since all options resulted in equal impact to the customer) and
5. Reverse (these reflected a customer's preferences not to experience an option due to its negative impact on them)

The Kano model was created in the early '80s by Japan's professor Noriaki Kano and continues today to be an essential tool for all organizations independent of industry or size.

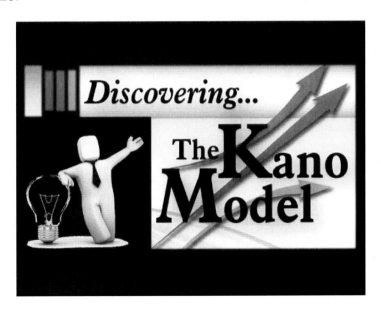

The Kano Model is:

Figure 1 – Satisfaction Execution Axis

Not all customer requirements have the same ability to deliver high satisfaction when done well. Now this sounds rather obvious, but there is a distinction Kano discovered that is worth noting. You could have two customer needs that are equally important, and one will cause high satisfaction when done well and the other will leave the customer neutral when done well.

To further illustrate, one customer requirement could be far more important than another requirement, but if they are both executed very well the less important one may be able to increase satisfaction far more than the more important requirement. This is because the two requirements fall into two different categories, each which has a different influence on delivering increased customer satisfaction. For example, take the brakes and fuel efficiency of your car.

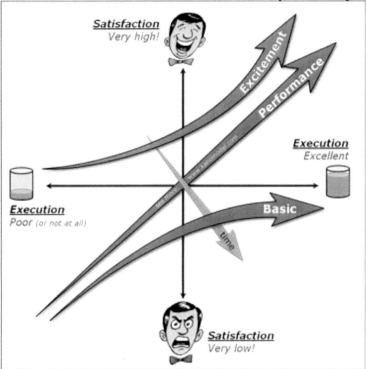

Kano 5 universal categories:

1. **Performance** - They are the most visible of the model's requirements

2. **Basic** - Must-bes'

3. **Excitement** - unexpected and pleasant surprises or delights. These are the innovations you bring into your offering.

4. **Indifferent** - customers simply don't care if they are present or absent.

5. **Reverse** - cause dissatisfaction when present and satisfaction when absent.

98 Sustaining profits and doing the right thing!

- To communicate 5 universal categories of customer requirements that all product and service developers need to be aware of in order to remain competitive.
- To show how each of these 5 universal categories can influence satisfaction and dissatisfaction.
- To show how 2 of the categories add value and 2 of the categories detract from value, and 1 of the categories creates new value.
- To help organizations understand their customer needs better than their customers understand their own needs.
- To provide a mechanism to help organizations understand and classify all potential customer requirements or features into these 5 categories so they can prioritize development efforts on the things that most influence satisfaction and loyalty. This is done by the Kano Survey or sometimes called a Kano Analysis.

Go to https://www.kanomodel.com/ and look at the videos.

One day in Japan, we had dinner together near Dr. Kano's home. He pointed out near a river and said, *"When home often I would walk along the banks of the river with bags and a trash pick-up stick and collect the trash."* Here was a world-famous professor fully setting up an example for us to follow.

24. Customer service teams are focused on providing the best possible customer experience and continuing customer relationships once a product is sold

1. They also specialize in customer retention and solve complex issues frustrating customers.

2. The customer service team is the face of the company, the front-line when customers contact a business for assistance.

Putting your staff into active teams is a wonderful idea. Working and learning together to find better and better ways to serve your customers.

25.   Honest advertising

Now this is a challenge. How do you say and write things that are absolutely honest? You want the customer to buy so you say things that they want to hear not necessary precisely what the product can deliver.

Can you meet the challenge? Advertisers write copy that appeals to customers wants and needs but does not always conform to what the product can deliver. For example, the major mobile phone companies all advertise 5G, but there is no 5G in my area and with my latest vendor there are areas where I do not even get 1G - I get no service at all.

In advertising, we exaggerate the benefit, and we conveniently say nothing about the negative sides of the product.

It is enjoyable to read an ad for a new drug:

"It is new wonder drug with just a few small side effects: "Swelling of legs, hands and feet; capillary leak syndrome; fever; muscle pain; unusual bruising; dizziness, blurry vision; rash; hives; blisters; nervous system and blood disorders; lymphoma; swollen tongue; dry mouth; weight gain; inability to fight infections; nausea, diarrhea; constipation; **depression***; dehydration;* **suicidal thoughts***. Oh, and death."*

Sustaining profits and doing the right thing!

Boy, we must be desperate to take that new medicine.

When younger, I smoked three packs a day.

Sit down and start to write honest ads and then give them to friends and family to read.

26.   The best cookies in the world

At Tokyo station there is a store selling Press Butter Sand cookies.

To get the cookies, you have to buy a ticket to get into the station and then you stand on-line to buy them. I believe there is always a line of people waiting.

It is well worth the wait. They are delicious and not too expensive. They are wonderful, not too sugary like many cookies.

The old saying, **"Bake a better cookie and the world will come to your door."**

30.   You never punish an employee who goes out of their way for the customer.

Marc Eugenio was stuck at a Clackamas, Oregon, gas station on Christmas Eve without enough money to

102 Sustaining profits and doing the right thing!
fill his tank after his paycheck was held at U.S. Bank. Emily James, right, a banker at a U.S. Bank call center, was fired after she drove to the station and gave him $20 from her own money.

"At U.S. Bank, we have policies and procedures in place to protect our customers and employees," the statement read. "Ms. James was terminated following an internal investigation into her interactions with a customer. During this review it was determined Ms. James did not use the available solutions to remedy the customer's situation and instead put herself and the bank at risk with her actions."

It took one month for the president of US Bank to reverse the bank's earlier decision. (I canceled my US Bank credit card.)

Chapter V - Investing in our employees

Investing in our employees. This starts with compensating them fairly and providing important benefits. It also includes supporting them through training and education that help develop new skills for a rapidly changing world. We foster diversity and inclusion, dignity and respect.

"There must be a better way."

Remove fear from the workplace Let's recognize that fear exists. Most people feel isolated, alone, and at the mercy of their superiors. We can change that by:

104 Sustaining profits and doing the right thing!
(a) Focusing on people building their skills and capabilities.

Robots easily replace unskilled labor not the highly skilled.

In the 1800's, craftspeople thrived. People were primarily artisans or farmers each with very high skills. Look at the old buildings, furniture, etc. and you can see the wonderful skills of the artisan in them. Their added value gave character and enriched the lives of people using them.

"The energy of a skilled master is in the piece they create, and that energy permeates, can be felt and absorbed and does enrich our lives." - Rudi

Around 1900, Frederick Taylor, considered to be the father of industrial engineering, to improve productivity, originated the concept of simplifying work. Instead of an artisan building a whole product, Taylor divided the work where the worker would do very repetitive tasks over and over again. Henry Ford adapted the idea and set up the assembly line. Work went from the high skilled artisan to people doing the same thing over and over again every few minutes. Work became tedious and boring. Ford had to double the wages of the assemble workers to keep them.

But, from this new concept of simplifying work for the human being, Ford Motor became one of the largest and most successful companies in the world. And then on every other company did the same. Many companies became very large and very rich but work for most people took away their personal dignity, their very sense of value in their skill and in themselves. People came to work to make a living and looked elsewhere for their value.

From this new commitment by the 181 the Top American CEOs to not only search for "profits," but now also to be socially responsible; hopefully they will begin to look at improving the very nature of work. You can start!

In my quest to discover how Japan improved their productivity and quality, starting in 1981, I ran numerous study missions to Japan. I visited over 250 manufacturing plants. One in particular plant was Canon Camera. At first, I saw workers assembling small parts of the camera and then passing them off to the next worker. As the years progressed, I saw them assembling their products on an assembly line then to a conveyor belt. Each process entailed doing the same work over and over again every few minutes.

A few years ago, I visited a Canon plant in Toride, Japan and watched people assembling copiers working in manufacturing cells where each worker's job was expanded. Instead of doing the same task over and over again every few minutes, the worker might spend 30 minutes building an entire subset of the copier. In fact, there were 28 people at Canon, at that time, that were called "supermeisters" (super masters) and they were able to build the entire copier by themselves with over 1000 parts in around three hours. And at a 30% improvement in productivity with no loss in quality.

Sustaining profits and doing the right thing!

A supermeister at Canon

She said, "After I complete assembling the copier, I feel I just made another baby."

Volvo many years ago, had teams building the cars, but they stopped the system for it was not that productive. Canon has done it very effectively. Yes, people can do amazing things if properly trained. Re-look now at your employees with new "eyes," and begin to tap into the depths of their knowledge and abilities. They all have the potential of becoming masters. They need you to recognize that hidden potential and help them bring it out. Your investment in them will surely bring your company greater value.

This is great! Let us reverse the direction of the past 100 years and recognize that people do have unlimited potential if we encourage them to be more self-reliant and to pick a skill to master in their life.

Have them pick a goal to develop themselves; doing something that they can get passionate about that other people need. The best way to motivate people is to help them find a skill to become the best at and encourage them to continually grow. Challenge them to become the best in the world at it.

Recognize that your investment in people will give you the payback that you are looking for. It is not just being altruistic. As people grow their personal value, the value of the company grows. Believe this!

We don't really have a choice. Look closely at what Huawei has done to become one of the leading electronic companies in the world. They used to pay people 30 cents an hour and now, even with the American embargo of their products, they sell more mobile phones then Apple and lead the world with 5G. Their new P40 mobile phone will give "shock waves" to the industry.

Huawei set up their own corporate universities and invested very heavily to uplift people's skills. We must now wake up and face these challenges if we are to survive. This new commitment is coming at a right and necessary time.

At the invitation from Tsinghua University I visited Beijing, China in 1983, the capital of the country. I thought I was visiting a farm, very few paved roads, oxcarts in the streets, run down hotels and the food was terrible. The last time I visited, a few years ago, the cities I visited were the most modern in the world and the food was superb. Yes, they started with very "cheap" labor; copied everything they could from us, replicated it, produced "junky" products, but improved those products and took over world markets. They are a threat that we must meet and challenge.

(b)   **Copying is great as long as you learn and can apply that knowledge**

108Sustaining profits and doing the right thing!

Somehow, we live in a myth that copying is wrong. Every child learns from copying their parents and their siblings and then reaches into their own individuality.

Watch artists in the Louvre or other great museums; they sit for hours and days copying from the old masters. People at work also improve themselves by watching and copying from the master, the best person doing the job.

In the ninth grade, I was sitting in a History class when a fellow classmate, Gary, came over to me and said, *"Norman, why are you so sad?"* I said, *"Gary, I am sad because I go home after school and I do read the home assignment but when I come into the class the next day and take the test; I can't remember the answer."* Gary said, *"Norman I had the same problem, but I came up with the solution. I go home and as I read, I write the key ideas onto a small sheet of paper and put the paper into my shirt pocket. When I take the test, I look at the paper."* I then said, *"Gary that is a brilliant idea."*

That night I went home and did the exact same thing and wrote down the key ideas onto a small sheet of paper and put the paper into my shirt pocket. During the exam the next day, I couldn't remember what I read, and I looked at the small sheet of paper, but the teacher saw me, grabbed the paper and called me a *"cheater."* She told all of the other teachers and my name was now "mud."

Rick Zwirn ©, 06
N. Bodek

My English teacher told my friend Monroe to not play with me for I was going to turn out to be a *"criminal."* She even put into the yearbook, *"Norman Bodek is the student most likely to get ahead, because he needs one!"*

Well, I didn't turn out to be a criminal. From that *"dumb"* student, I was later in life to run a highly successful business and also teach at Portland State University.

I love to read books and I read at least one or two books a week, but I still have a poor memory from reading. Luckily, I have a very good memory for things I do and experience.

After World War II, thousands of Japanese came to America to learn from us and we graciously allowed them to come into our plants and watch us. After visiting they would say to the plant manager, *"Can I take your picture?"* And we would say yes and stand in front of a machine. The Japanese visitor would then ask us to kindly move over a little bit. They did not really want your picture; they wanted the technology; they wanted like the Chinese to replicate your machine and process. The Japanese were excellent in copying from us but then they made it even better.

Please don't be too shocked. Look, we want people to be successful and if copying helps them apply their knowledge than copying is good. With our current educational system, you can go through 13 years of grammar school and not have a skill to make a living. To me this it a crime, a terrible waste of human potential. If you would like to talk to me about this, call me at 360-737-1883 or email me at bodek@pcspress.com

(c) Support children to become mechanics

Germany is known for having the highest skilled mechanics driven by their apprenticeship program when young people choose between becoming a skilled mechanic versus going off to college. When I was younger in the 1940's, I had a choice to go to a trade school or to going towards academics. My parents chose for me to go on to college. That process to select trade versus academic is virtually gone in America.

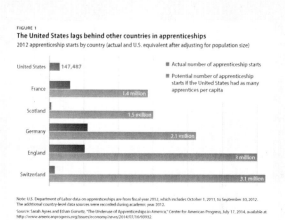

FIGURE 1
The United States lags behind other countries in apprenticeships
2012 apprenticeship starts by country (actual and U.S. equivalent after adjusting for population size)

Note: U.S. Department of Labor data on apprenticeships are from fiscal year 2012, which includes October 1, 2011, to September 30, 2012. The additional country-level data sources were recorded during academic year 2012.
Source: Sarah Ayres and Ethan Gurwitz, "The Underuse of Apprenticeships in America," Center for American Progress, July 17, 2014, available at http://www.americanprogress.org/issues/economy/news/2014/07/16/93932.

Today in America, fewer than 5 percent of young people train as apprentices, majority learn in the construction trades. In Germany, the number is closer to 60 percent—in fields as diverse as advanced manufacturing, IT, banking, and hospitality. And in Europe, what's often called *"dual training"* is a highly respected career path.

"Dual training captures the idea at the heart of every apprenticeship: Trainees split their days between classroom instruction at a vocational school and on-the-job time at a company. The theory they learn in class is reinforced by the practice at work. They also learn work habits and responsibility and, if all goes well, absorb the culture of the company. Trainees are paid for their time, including in class. The arrangement lasts for two to four years, depending on the sector. And both employer and employee generally hope it will lead to a permanent job—for employers, apprentices are a crucial talent pool. 'Lifelong learning' is still a distant dream for most Americans. In Germany, it's a reality." https://cutt.ly/fr5HbQI

I do hope as part of our new vision, American industry will start to help young people learn new skills for us to compete in the world.

Plan your training process and training courses. Envision the skills you might need in the future and offer the training to your workers.

(c) Encourage and allow people to be part of effective work teams

Most of us love college and professional sports. I do like football and recently watched the National Football Championship game between LSU and Clemson. A sellout crowd of 76,885 watched LSU defeat Clemson at the

112Sustaining profits and doing the right thing!
Mercedes-Benz Superdome in the title game; millions watched on TV.

We do love team sports

But for some strange reasons we do not love teams at work. We must change that attitude. There is enormous power for us when people are part of work teams.

Virtually, every large and medium size company in Japan has Quality Control Circles (QCC) to address quality issues. QCC is when a small group of workers, 5 to 8, get together to solve quality problems, maybe one or two problems a year. The groups are taught the quality tools to discover and correct the quality problems and they are taught how to present their conclusions. Japan went from making *"junk,"* to become the highest quality producers in the world and I think QCC teams had a lot to do with that happening.

One day, I was in the audience sitting next to the president of Juki Corporation, worlds' leader of industrial sewing machines, watching groups of QCC teams present their past successes. After one presentation, the president stood up, clapped, and congratulated the group. One woman said, *"We appreciate your support, but we don't want praise; we want to learn how to be better!"*

I was amazed at the response and wish workers in American felt so secure that they could do the same.

When I started my newsletter, Productivity, in 1980 I wrote in the first newsletter about Quality Control Circles. I met Wayne Riker, who was the first American manager, at Lockheed, to use quality control circles and he gave me a copy of all of his training material to use in the newsletter. Wayne, left Lockheed, opened his own consulting company to teach Quality Control Circles. Wayne was very successful, and many America corporations had QCC activities going, but almost all of the companies stopped having them. It was a mistake. QCC teaches the employees how to use the quality tools to solve quality problems. It allows all of them to be their own inspectors. It takes the burden away from the Quality manager. I believe that every top Japanese company still has quality control circles.

I recommend you change your patterns. Rethink how you can put people into teams to solve quality problems. Being part of a team could be highly motivating. Teach them and give them the quality tools they need to do a better job. Every quality manager knows these basic QC tools - teach them to all of the workers.

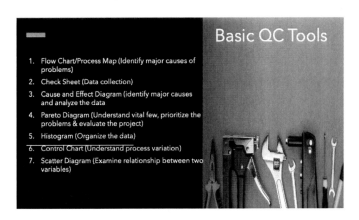

Basic QC Tools

1. Flow Chart/Process Map (Identify major causes of problems)
2. Check Sheet (Data collection)
3. Cause and Effect Diagram (identify major causes and analyze the data
4. Pareto Diagram (Understand vital few, prioritize the problems & evaluate the project)
5. Histogram (Organize the data)
6. Control Chart (Understand process variation)
7. Scatter Diagram (Examine relationship between two variables)

114Sustaining profits and doing the right thing!

There are many reasons why American managers do not encourage team activities. One of which is the fear of losing your power to the team, but we must change that attitude and allow people to work and learn from each other. Let the people working for you become smarter than you. It will only cause you to grow.

(d) We are not *"rugged individuals."* It is a myth

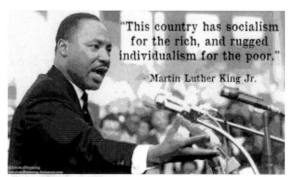

"This country has socialism for the rich, and rugged individualism for the poor."
— Martin Luther King Jr.

It might have existed in the age when cowboys roamed the range, but we are not cowboys today. Today we need each other for support.

It is a myth that supports the current system. Yes, we all do have opportunities to grow, but we want to allow everyone to have that opportunity.

(e) Design work for human beings

Years back, I visited a new Ford Motor Engine Plant near Detroit, Michigan. They had spent two billion dollars buying the latest machines from Germany. As I walked along the assembly area, I saw the new machines and workers sitting at the side reading newspapers. Ford had invested in machines not in the people. People were just slotted in.

Investment in training workers was perceived as reducing profits and was drastically reduced. In this new commitment to **"help develop new skills for a rapidly changing world,"** we clearly have to see the valued added in investing in people and how this will lead to new growth opportunities.

Sustaining profits and doing the right thing!

This is good. This is also very good.

Do it! Write down a large list of reasons why you want to design work differently.

3. Manager's and supervisor's roles must change from command and control to become coaches to develop people to their fullest

The old chess games

This is the heart of it - the real heart of this new commitment. One day, I visited a Pepsi Cola plant in Texas invited to talk about Total Productive Maintenance (TPM). They heard about this new TPM, but they really only wanted to know how it would improve profits not how it could make processing more effective. They were very good in their focus on finding ways to improve profits. I was living in   another world and could not teach them.

We must develop new training courses to first teach managers and supervisors to gain trust from their employees that the new commitment is sincere - that as the employees gain new skills the company can get richer.

Virtually every great athlete has a coach. Every great sport's team has a coach. A year ago, in Columbus, Ohio I keynoted a conference for the Chief Executive Network Organization, and I asked the audience of 250 people, 100 were CEO's, if they had coaches. They all agreed. Yes, almost every top CEO in America has at least one coach to support them to help them lead the company,   but very few workers, employees, have coaches. We know this, but there has been a *"myth"* that coaching is expensive. I know that almost everyone can be a coach to someone else. (Read the interview with Kazuyoshi Hisano later in the book.)

I visited Chugai Pharmaceutical in Japan, and every new employee gets a coach, an older worker, to meet with them every day to review to see that they are attaining their goals. It is not complicated. People are asked to write down their tasks on a Daily Diary, to review them each to see if they attained them, to write ways to improve (what would you do differently, if you could today all over again,) and to write questions for their coach.

The coach reviews the Daily Diary with the worker and is there to support them, to help them to complete their tasks and attain their goals. They are very positive in their feedback and are very careful with criticism.

118**Sustaining profits and doing the right thing!**

A teacher gives information; a consultant and a manager tells you what to do, but a coach knows how to ask questions to have you come up with your own answers to do the job correctly.

4.   Education in America must also change

If we are to stay competitive, we must begin to change our education system entirely. I believe it is archaic.

An investment in knowledge always pays the best interest

-Benjamin Franklin

I went through 13 years of grammar school and graduated without a skill. This a tragedy for young children. We have to learn how to read, count and write, but most of the other courses to me were a waste of time and I hated it. I have never needed to use geometry, trigonometry, calculus, and languages: French, Spanish, and German never stayed in my head and frankly most of the other courses I have never used. I could surely have used carpentry, electricity, cooking, marriage and raising a family, outdoor survival skills, proper exercise and diet, etc. Most school systems developed their curriculum around what they perceive industry needs. Industry has to take some greater responsibility to influence change in our educational system. We need people to be educated, self-reliant, goal oriented, creative and highly skilled.

I taught for a number of years at the Business School at Portland State University and often wondered how the students got here. Many were not motivated or qualified. And, being at the school wasn't really going to help them in their future.

I went through 13 years of grammar school, six years of college and never had a "goal." No teacher ever asked me to pick something to help me be successful in life. I had no star in front of me. I had no vision of what future could look like.

My father was an accountant, not rich at all, but was able to make a living and afforded to send my brother and I to college without taking any loans. I also did not have to take out any loans as I went to graduate school and beyond. I also was fortunate to be able to pay for the higher education for my two daughters

I graduated without the burden of any loans while my grandson Anthony and his wife Sonja owed over $125,000. I did help them but surely not enough. In 1955, tuition at Harvard was less than $1,000 per year while today it is close to $50,000 or more per year. Okay, cost of living has gone up eight times since 1955 meaning Harvard at today's dollars should cost around $8,000 per year not $50,000. Something happened drastically. I don't think the quality of education has increased to that extent.

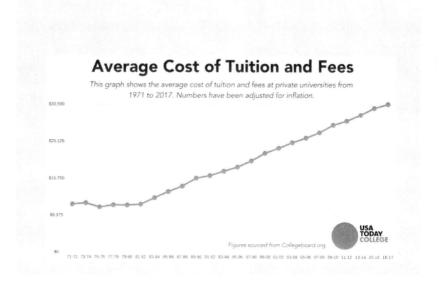

Average Cost of Tuition and Fees

This graph shows the average cost of tuition and fees at private universities from 1971 to 2017. Numbers have been adjusted for inflation.

Figures sourced from Collegeboard.org.

USA TODAY COLLEGE

With the cost of education rising substantially, corporate America also reduced investment in training of their employees, because their focus was solely on profits.

Yes, Larry Fink, the 181 US corporations, and the 30 Global corporations have opened a new "pandora's box. *"We should pursue the "whole hog,"* and look at what is really possible for us. I don't want pablum. I want our society to be great giving everyone the possibly to grow. Let us imagine a great new world.

Luckily, when younger it came to me that **"If *someone else could do it, so could I."*** I might not become as good as Tiger Woods or be as good as many others, but I surely could be the best me.

"An investment in knowledge always pays the best interest." — Benjamin Franklin

5.   People need real respect

The old way!

Toyota had two "pillars for their success: Just-in-Time and Jidoka. Jidoka a Japanese word that relates to impowering every worker to stop working when they detect a quality problem. Toyota does not want the problem to be passed to the next worker. When a worker detects a problem, they can pull a cord which alerts others, causes the supervisor to immediately come over to help and can stop the entire assembly line. I saw this done several times at Toyota in

122Sustaining profits and doing the right thing!

Japan where one person stopped the entire line. This gives tremendous respect to that one worker. Toyota changed the name of that pillar from Jidoka to Respect for People.

But what really gives people respect and is Toyota a prime example? Toyota is very good, but Toyota still has a 3-4-minute takt time - takt time is a German for "Clock or Beat," representing the time given to each worker or process to do the job. A three-minute takt time would allow around 150 cars to be   manufactured on one shift. This means that the worker will do approximately the thing on every car every three minutes. Is this real respect?

We already mentioned what Canon was doing; Honda in Thailand manufacturing automobiles has set up a new assembly line with the worker up on the platform. Instead the of worker standing in front of the moving line doing repetitive work, they are now up on the platform making an entire sub-set of the vehicle. This idea is spreading to expand people's work, to make work more challenging and interesting without reducing productivity or quality.

In World War II, the German navy was blocking Great Britain from receiving oil   from abroad. Coal was the source of Great Britain's energy. England needed men to mine the coal and also go to war. Eric Trist was at the Tavistock Institute and was asked to discover which mines were the most productive. He found one   particular mine was way ahead of all the others. This mine only had production workers: no supervisors, no secretaries, no accountants, no HR people, no nurses, etc. They were self-organized and without any supervision.

From this discovery, Eric Trist with Albert Cherns and Lou Davis created the concept of Socio-technical design on how to modernize manufacturing to make sure that work was good both for technology and for people. Lou Davis was a professor at UCLA and often spoke at one of my conferences. One day, he visited my office in Connecticut and noticed I was still involved in data entry and said, *"Keypunching was not a job for a human being."*

Lou taught a number of consultants "Socio-tech;" these consultants went out and taught Socio-tech to a number of American plants and these plants were probably the most productive in America. Unfortunately, the companies did not know how to spread Socio-tech to their other plants.

The problem was that companies might have had one plant but did not know how to spread it throughout their organization. I always felt that if a company with Socio-tech and JIT; they would be world-class.

In the early 1980's Toyota wanted to come to America to manufacture automobiles but they were a little fearful of not being accepted. So, they approached Ford Motor with a

Sustaining profits and doing the right thing!
proposition to take over one of their plants to teach them the
Toyota Production System, (JIT.) Ford, foolishly, refused.

Toyota then approached General Motors with the same
idea and GM agreed, but they gave Toyota their worst plant
to run in Freemont, California; the one with the most difficult
union and probably the lowest productivity of all of their plants.

Toyota started to run the plant in 1984 and only one
year later the plant, call NUMMI, went from the lowest rated
to the highest,) I think GM had then around 200 plants.
NUMMI was great and allowed Toyota to learn to manage
American workers and Toyota subsequently opened their
plant in Kentucky, but unfortunately, GM could not spread the
knowledge from NUMMI to any of their other plants and a few
years later GM went bankrupt.

I do recommend you learn more about Socio-tech and
also more about the Toyota Production System.

6.   **No Horenso**

Horenso is *"spinach"* in Japanese. It is a prevalent term
meaning before you do something new you should:

Ho - report your idea to someone else, to your
supervisor, or to your group,
Ren - communicate your idea with others before
you implement it and
So - consult with others before doing something
new.

Japanese management is often called "consensual or
consensus." They want you to discuss your idea with others
before you implement it. It is as if a group of brains is better

than one alone. This is also true in America whenever you want to do something new that might cause the company spending more money, you check it out with a superior. It is not self-reliant. It is a cautious way to manage, but is it a necessary practice?

However, there is one company in Japan where Horenso is not permitted. Akio Yamada was the president of Mirai Industry and insisted on No Horenso. He said, if you want to do something new and different than do it on your own. *"Trust yourself"* he said, *"You know your work better than anyone else. You don't have to discuss it or ask for permission."* It is a very unusual management style but Mirai is probably the most successful company in the world for a company with around 1000 employees. More patents, higher salary, more vacation days, less workdays than anyone else. He said, *"If you make a mistake, we will give you $6 for every mistake, but don't ever make the same mistake again."*

I published Yamada's book The Happiest Company to Work for. You can get the book for free on Amazon Kindle if you have their unlimited membership. Listed in the book is around 100 ideas that make the company the happiest to work for. Many of the ideas might appear to be radical, but if Mirai can do it - than why can't you?

Some ideas are:

1. You must differentiate - If you can only make the same thing others do, then don't sell it even if it makes money. *"Mirai Industry makes something different. We do not make the same product that other companies make."*

2. No sales quota

3. Everyone is fulltime

4. There is no such thing as the supervisor forcing me to do something

5. If an employee thinks a business trip is necessary, then they send an invoice to the accounting section and just go

6. We let people make decisions based on their experience

7. If a company can't pay a decent salary to allow its employees to live a life happily, nor pay taxes to contribute to the society, it is almost worthless

8. Our focus is to make workers happy

9. We don't make it cheaper, in fact we want to see it at a high price

10. No carrot and stick

11. No gifts to customers

12. Very little investment in new equipment

13. Every five years everyone goes on overseas trip. When I was there everyone, all 1000 employees went to Italy for one week

14. Yamada emphasizes that company owners need to know that every worker has potential, and in order to help them fulfill their potential, the company must give them a chance and good treatment. When employees realize that they are receiving special treatment, they will demonstrate a remarkable ability.

15. Mirai never lost money in over 50 years

16. At other companies the upper management are the thinkers, set policies and others receive and follow orders and do the job. But this is not an efficient way for the company. Better that thinking is done by everyone – to think also makes work more fun. Just doing the job and task is not enjoyable. We encourage people to think, to be engaged, to be enthusiastic and we have many things to inspire them.

17. What if you fail? The supervisor will say, *"Good job, you thought it through,"* no scolding. *"I compliment you for trying."* Manager's job is to watch what are the likely events that might fail to prevent problems. *"Hold on, maybe there is a different way,"* – a dialog takes place that makes it easier to work here.

18. Too many rules might damage creativity.

19. Turnover last year was 1.7%, a high number for us. Average in Japan is 5%. (US companies had an average 22% turnover rate*

20. They get around 10,000 ideas per year, average of 10 implement ideas per   year per person

Sustaining profits and doing the right thing!

21. Don't treat people as a cost

22. Easy to work here but a challenge to the managers

23. Why are we doing these things: not to be famous but to motivate employees to feel enthusiastic to work hard and come up with new ideas

Of course, many of the above ideas are challenging but as you read them ask yourself, *"is it possible for us?"*

7. People are the real assets of a company

"Boss, I am so happy to follow you."

Often when I keynote a conference, I ask the audience what is your most important asset? Invariably, they say people, but people are not listed on the balance sheet and when you invest in people, you must expense it even though the benefits are derived in the future. When you buy a machine, you can put it on the balance sheet and write it off over many years. As we said earlier, our accounting principles are archaic and do not help the long-term benefits for the organization. HP has laid off over 120,000 people in the last few years and even a month ago added another 5000. It is crazy! People are your most important asset but for short-term profits they become expendable. I predict HP will shortly be gone. (Ironically, last week Xerox upped an offer to buy HP.)

So, now, look at people that work for you differently. Look at them as real assets to be trained and developed. Treat them right and they will work their "tail off," for you.

8.   Everyone needs a coach

In 1979, I started Productivity Inc. - Press and published over 250 management books of which 100 were Japanese translations including the books of Taiichi   Ohno and Dr. Shigeo Shingo, co-creators of the Toyota Production System (Lean management.) Miraculously, for several reasons: I was the dumbest student in the 9th grade. In the yearbook that year you will see under my name the message, *"Norman is the student to most likely get a head, because he needs one."* The English teacher surely did not like me, also I cannot read Japanese. I do trust my *"gut,"* and many people in Japan helped.

One of my latest discoveries is Takashi Harada who was a junior high school track and field coach at the lowest rated school in Osaka. His students lived in the slums and it was very hard for him to motivate them to become achievers. To get into high school, at the time, the students either had to pass a test, very few did, or pay the fees; very few families could afford them, or the student could get   an   athletic scholarship. Harada focused on the later. After studying for 20 years the world's best coaches and educational systems he derived his Harada Method and in the next six years 12 students won 13 gold medals (meaning they were the best athlete at their age in their athletic discipline in all of Japan.)

Sustaining profits and doing the right thing!
The   school also went from the lowest rated to the highest both athletically and academically Harada became very famous. A few years later, he opened his own consulting firm and over 90,000 people have been taught the method.

The Harada Method has you decide what you want in life and to pick a goal to attain those wants and then to create 64 tasks, steps, to take you to your goal. Each day you take one or more of your tasks, schedule to do it on a Daily Diary, evaluate yourself on your accomplishment and work with a coach to insure you do it.

Tiger Woods has a coach. Virtually every great athlete and every great team has a coach; and I repeat every CEO I believe has a coach and I have spoken with   many, but the average person at work who desperately needs encouragement does not have a coach. Yes, they do have a supervisor or a manager, but they most often play another role. A coach is there to support you, to observe you and to help develop you to your fullest while most managers are there to monitor to see that you are doing the job properly.

The Harada Method teaches you how to work with a coach and also how to become a coach for others. It is not complicated. Every person can learn how to coach another person. I developed a Harada Method APP for the iPhone. You might like to check it out.

Go To App Store and Have Fun Planning Your Life!

9.   Pay people well

In 1970, the average CEO from America's top corporations made around 20 times the average worker. Today it is close to 300 times. This week as I am writing this book, Dennis Muilenburg, the CEO of The Boeing Company was interrogated by US Congressmen and was criticized for receiving 30 million dollars last year. He replied, *"The board of directors decided on his compensation, not him."* Now, we are not at all criticizing the CEO's for their compensation. They surely deserve huge salaries and bonuses leading these top corporations, but they should treat their employees fairly and let them share in the corporation's success.

Yes, all the things recommend in this book will cost more money initially and   increased costs will reduce profits, but as you add value and build skills the result   should   be more profits not less.

Recently, I saw on Netflix the documentary American Factory about Fuyao a Chinese company that bought a

Sustaining profits and doing the right thing!
closed GM factory to make auto glass in America. The plant went from 10,000 people to 2000, from $29 per hour to $12 (raised to $14.). We saw people working in their plant in China and in Dayton, Ohio. It was a shock! The Americans all looked overweight and worked at half the pace of the Chinese. However, the Chinese were patient and went from a six-month loss of 40 million to a profit. The film is a "wake up call." Watch it and figure out how you can help the American worker to succeed.

10. **No carrot and stick**

Treat people with respect. Carefully select new people and create a climate where workers share the responsibility to get the job done correctly. Interview new employees carefully. Challenge them. Inspire them. Tell them your expectations and treat them properly.

11. **Let people make decisions and become problem solvers - encourage   creativity and innovation from everyone**

In 1898, Kodak started the first suggestion system and the first idea submitted was *"clean the windows."* A simple but great idea. However, back then the worker was not allowed to implement their own idea. They could not leave their job. So, the burden of implementing went to the supervisor who felt they already had enough to do. The suggestion system quickly went from an employee empowering system to get improvement ideas from everyone to a cost saving system; the worker received 10% of the savings, but the average company in America only received one new idea every seven years from the average worker.

Around 1970, the Japanese copied the American Suggestion System and Toyota, for example, received one idea per employee that year. However. the Japanese went back to Kodak's original idea, of involving all workers in continuous improvement, and having the worker who discovered the problem come up with a solution and then implement it. Within a short period of time the workers understood and started to come up with many small improvements that they could implement. Subsequently, I published a book titled 40 Years 20 Million Ideas the Toyota Suggestion System, about Toyota in the 1980s getting on the average of 70 implemented ideas per employee per year, and inspiring workers. Most of them were very small ideas but it saved Toyota multi-millions of dollars.

I wrote a few books on the Japanese suggestion system with Bunji Tozawa, president of the HR Association in Japan. One book was called The Idea Generator. Subsequently, I taught the system called Quick and Easy Kaizen to American companies, one of which was Technicolor Corporation in Detroit. We asked all of the production workers to look around their work area, find small problems and come up with solutions to those problems that they could implement on their own. Within only one year the workers implemented over 20,000 ideas saving their plant millions of dollars. Not only the money, but it generated real new excitement in their work.

134Sustaining profits and doing the right thing!

Michael Miller was an employee at Technicolor whose job was to simply close the cover of the video cassettes as they moved along the line. He did thousands   a   day. Michael on his own very cleverly figured out, by simply using cardboard   and   tape   how   to   have   the   covers   close automatically without him. Michael had *"Put himself out of a job."* Luckily, he had no fear and was then given something much more creative to do.

Quick & Easy TIP	
Before Improvement	**After Improvement**
ONE PERSON STANDING closing TOP OF MULTI PACK	I PUT CORNER ON CONVEYER SO iT CAN CLOSE By iT SELF ALiMiNATE ONE PERSON
The Effect: CLOSE BOXES By iT SELF, SAVE PERSON And moNEY	
Date: 1-17-02 **Name:** Michael Mills	

What can happen when you empower your employees?

People have wonderful ideas if management can only learn to ask for them. Each idea is small but when you implement thousands of these small ideas the result can be as powerful as inventing a new technology. We all always looking for the exotic when we can get so much more from involving all of the employees in improvement activities. If you want continuous improvement than get all employees involved.

The Kaizen Suggestion System - Quick and Easy Kaizen

With Kaizen, you change, the workplace changes.

Steps for Kaizen:

1) Attention—Find a problem. "Why! Something strange! Can I do anything about it?"
2) Investigation—Find a cause. "Why is it this way? Why does it happen?"
3) Idea Generation—Generate an idea. "How about this? This method might work?"
4) Judgment—Consider various conditions. "Does it work this way? Am I missing something important?"
5) Implementation—Implement a Kaizen. "Let's try it. Let's do it if it can be done easily."
6) Follow-up—Confirm the results. "Let's check the results. Let's follow it up until the results are desirable.

QUICK & EASY TIP

Before : The Skids were not placed in one location where the associates could find them when needed.

After : Made a Board that identified where the skids were to be placed.

QUICK & EASY TIP

Before : The Paper holder is a safety hazard to the Associates working on the Ship stations.

After : The Direction of the Paper holder is changed and is no longer a safety hazard to the associates working on the ship stations.

The Key Board Stand was Obstructing People Working on the Ship Station	The Key Board Stand was removed and hence No More Obstruction.

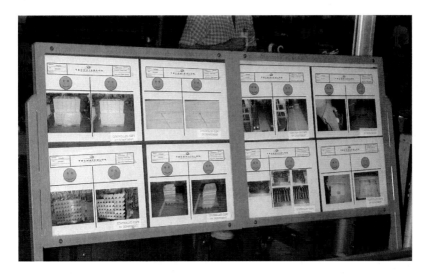

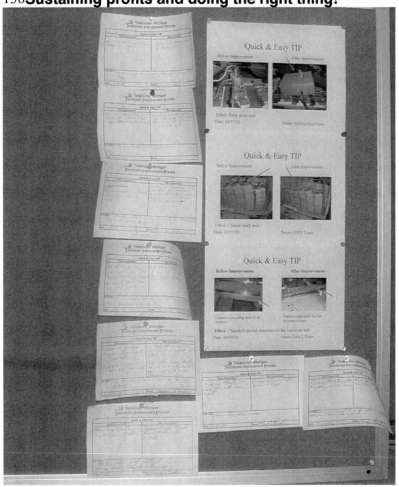

I made a major mistake

One day, after teaching Quick and Easy Kaizen for a few years, I got a telephone call from the owner of a small manufacturing plant outside of Pittsburgh who said, *"Norman, I want you to teach my employees the Japanese suggestion system, but I can't afford you."* I immediately said, *"Yes you can, only pay me 30% of the savings from the first year."* He jumped at the option and invited me to come out. There were around 150 employees in the company.

I initially trained around 30 of their employees on how to discover problems, take a picture of them, write up a possible solution to the problems, implement them and then take another picture showing the solution. A few weeks later, I returned to teach another group but when I looked at my client, I saw one of the saddest faces I had ever seen. I said foolishly, *"Forget about the deal. Write me a check for $35,000 instead."* He jumped at the offer.

Subsequently, we visited the plant floor and stopped in front of one worker. I said Tim, *"Please show me one of your ideas."* He said, *"Norman, I am a polisher and my job is to use this machine to polish metal plates. I earlier put one plate on a fixture and placed it against the polisher and allowed it to polish the plate. I asked someone to help me make a fixture that could hold two plates at the same time. We did it. Now I can polish two plates at the same time it took me to do one in the past."* Simple but a very powerful idea.

If we take an average labor cost plus overhead of around $40,000, I would have received 30% or $12,000 from that one idea. And the plant received over 1,500 ideas that year. I foolishly gave up over $1,000,000.

12.   **Mindfulness**

Earlier in my life, I was an atheist and did not follow any religion or believe in any God. Then I almost died, lost a kidney due to a very bad doctor who operated poorly. I was out of work for around four months. One day, a young man, a Jehovah Witness, rang the doorbell and wanted to teach me the bible. Since I had not read the bible before, I allowed him to do it. After the session, he wanted to give me the bible for free. I said, *"No, charge me something."* Well I gave him a dollar and for the first time in my life, at age 35, I read the entire bible, around 1100 hundred pages. At first, I was very confused for the bible was a history book filled with many terrible things, people killing each other. I never imagined the bible to be like that, but it opened my curiosity and I started to study more closely what religion was all about. Believe it or not but every Sunday for a year, I took my wife and two daughters to a different church, temple, etc. I liked it   but my children actually hated it. I continued to search until I discovered Yoga Meditation.

Mindfulness is a process of bringing one's attention to experiences occurring in   the   present   moment   without judgement. It appears to reduce depression,   stress,   and anxiety.   Even though every religion has some form of mindfulness, I would attribute the original concept to the teachings of the Buddha who said, *"You should focus your mind within, on your breath inside your body, and begin to realize the ultimate truth."*

When you do meditate, you actually learn to relax and to accept life differently. You learn to be more compassionate to yourself and to others. Mindfulness helps you to reduce your stress.

13.   **Provide everyone with medical coverage**

I believe everyone in Europe is covered medically. Canadians are covered. Why are we different? We are all educated for free through high school, shouldn't we do the same and give people free medical coverage? The United States is ranked in last place on health care from the leading

11 countries and we spend almost double what other advanced countries spend.

I once needed colchicine, a medication for my Gout, and I went to a drug store in England and paid $5.00 for a bottle. Colchicine has been around for over 1000 years and used to cost around 10 cents a pill in America. The FDA took colchicine off the market, gave a monopoly to the maker of Colcrys, a new name for colchicine, but now sells for around $7 per pill.

From my own personal experiences, I could write a whole book on the problems with our medical system: 50% of doctors are burned out, virtually all decisions must be made by the doctor, very little empowerment to nurses, technicians and staff, 450,000 people die yearly of medical error, an estimated 530,000 families turn to bankruptcy each year because of medical issues and bills, lack of medical insurance for millions of people, enormous waste of time with billing and insurance claims, the opioid crises (45,000 die each year from overdose), shortage of nurses, and very few are taught about self-care.

With the new commitment to be more socially responsible, we should relook at this health care issue. Corporations can have an enormous power to help improve healthcare in America. What kind of educational programs can you provide for your employees?

14.   **Believe in the theory that human nature is fundamentally good**

For example, when telling an employee to do a certain task, don't think that the employee will cheat you about it. Believe all employees are good-natured.

142 Sustaining profits and doing the right thing!

This is a challenge in our country for some people are not honest but to run a socially reliable company we have to find a way to trust everyone. In my life, I have always, on meeting new people, trusted them and I have often gotten burnt, Sure, I should be more careful who I trust, but I don't want to inflict a past problem on new people I meet.

15.   Miracles do happen - stay open

In 1960, I was an accountant working with my father and brother in the Bronx,   New York City. My office was my automobile. My father set up the accounting practice, but he never even graduated high school. Somehow, he took a few bookkeeping courses at Columbia University and found a number of immigrants and became their accountant. He kept their books and made out their tax returns and was able to make a decent living sending both my brother and I to college.

I would visit a carpenter, electrician or metal working shop for around three to four hours and take the client's checks and enter them into these large ledgers, for around $15 per month. It was tedious and boring work. I was married with one daughter and was grateful to have a job, so I did it.

Magically, one day my father noticed an article in the New York Times about a company not too far away using a Bendix G15 computer to do sales analysis.

This was before IBM had their computers. My brother immediately encouraged me to go with him to visit the company. At the company, we asked them if they could help us automate our practice. It was only a dream for we had no money to spend.

A few weeks later, they called us to come back and told us that they did not have the knowledge to automate our accounting work but suggested we form a new company together; we would teach them; they would write the software programs we could sell the services to others. It was a miracle. We struggled but miraculously discovered how to use a Friden Ad-Punch calculator to enter in the   date,   dollar amount and a general ledger number for each check.

Sustaining profits and doing the right thing!

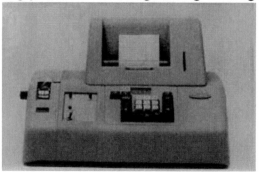

At first, we had the Bendix G15 read the tape and then punch out IBM cards to read on an IBM 101 accounting machine to print out the accounting reports.

Subsequently, we bi-passed the G15 and went to an IBM keypunch machine to convert the tape to IBM cards.

We then sorted the IBM cards:

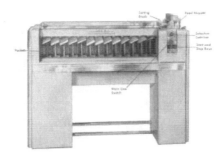

Then printed the cards on a large IBM 101 accounting machine:

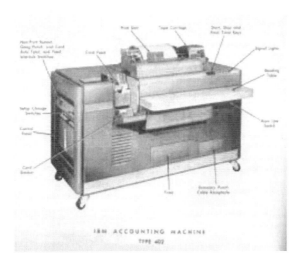

As the general ledger report was printed, we also punched out summary cards from an attached IBM card punch machine.

146Sustaining profits and doing the right thing!

Figure 4. IBM 1402 Card Read-Punch

Then the summary cards were used to print out the beautiful financial reports. We did all of this and sold the reports to accountants for $7.50 per month.

My brother and I worked during the days as accountants and at night worked at various places at night: at a butcher distributer in the Bronx and at Woolworth's machine center.

I believe we were the first people in the world to automate accounting.

Instead of sitting in the job shops for half a day for $15.00, we visited the companies, maybe six in a day, picked up their checks and took it to our new office where our assistant would enter the checks into the Friden Add-Punch.

Part of the miracle, Macy's needed our tape to card machine to convert their customer name and address tapes and flooded us with enough business that my brother and I were able to leave our father's practice. He didn't need us anymore as we produced all his reports for his clients. We set up Tape Accounting Center and with the help of Friden and Burroughs salespeople, we acquired many accounting firms to service.

In fact, a few years later. ADP offered to buy us out and offered us 7% of their stock. We weren't smart enough to accept, only worth over two billion today.

Instead of trusting Jimny Cricket, we trusted the wrong people and even though we were 20 years ahead of Bill Gates we didn't turn out to become billionaires.

15.   We encourage everyone to grow and to do their best

I had an amazing teacher, Rudi, once tell me to always ask inside myself to grow. Often, we ask for things that have a limited life. Our goals might be attained but then what. When you focus solely on growth the opportunities are endless. I am now 87 and still have the same wish to continuously grow until I discover the ultimate truth.

We hope that everyone can come to work highly motivated to do a superior job and continuously learn and grow. Management's role is to support that process.

If you improve your skills, you have a greater chance to have a marvelous life. I feel everyone should pick some skill that serves others and become a master at it.

16.   Set up study groups

148Sustaining profits and doing the right thing!

Probably the most powerful and least expensive way to train people is to set up book study groups.

In 1981, I lead my second two-week study mission to Japan to discover why they were so advanced in productivity and quality. In the group was Jack Warne, senior vice president of Omark Industries, the leading manufacturer in America in saw chains. During the first week, Jack was highly skeptical and said after each plant visit, *"I don't understand at all what the Japanese are doing; my Omark plants were much better."* Of course, as the leader of the group, I was embarrassed.

However, on the second Tuesday we visited a Nippondenso plant, a major supplier to Toyota. The plant manager Mr. Ohta said, *"We have seven hours' worth of raw materials inventory, nine hours of work in process, and eight hours of finished goods. . . . We feed 10 auto plants, making deliveries every two hours, and, in the last five years, we've held up one product line for 30 minutes."*

The claims bordered on the miraculous, and Warne was appropriately skeptical. until he visited the shop floor. and eventually Jack was impressed and said, *"I'm an old tool-and-die man, and once I got out onto the plant, I understood what was really happening."* The revelation was nothing short of amazing. *'It was like being born again. I thought, God Almighty, this is the secret of their productivity."* (Go the Internet and enter "Omark and Inc Magazine 1984 to read all about Omark's Lean journey)

Rick Zwirn © ,02
N. Bodek

As we were leaving the plant Mr. Ohta gave us a sheet of paper and printed on it was, The Study of the Toyota Production System from an Engineering Viewpoint, by Shigeo Shingo from Japan Management Association (JMA). I had no idea what it meant, but on arriving in Tokyo from Nagoya I called JMA and they told me it was a book in English. I told my group of around 12 members but only Jack and I wanted a copy. I bought the two books and Jack and I did the exact same thing, independently, read the book on the airplane going home and bought 500 copies. Since this was the first book ever in English describing Just-In-Time, the Toyota Production System, I bought the copies to sell to my newsletter subscribers and Jack distributed his 500 to all his engineers and managers.

Learn Value Analysis and Value Engineering

Omark had an unusable ability as their engineers and managers had been trained in Value Analysis-Value Engineering techniques. They knew how to read a book in small study groups to take the most important information and get it   applied on their factory floor.   *"It isn't the easiest book in the world to read,"* confesses Larry White, plant manager of Omark's Oregon Saw Chain plant in Portland, which manufactures $50 million worth of saw chain, saw guide bars, and accessories a year. Intimidated by the challenge of Shingo's *"Janglish,"* a hybrid of Japanese and English, eight members of Oregon Saw's management divided and conquered. Each was responsible for reading and reporting on one chapter. *"It took us 32 hours to get through."*

We called this the *"Green Book."* The Omark small study groups asked each other, *"How can we apply this at Omark."* They did it and they did it very powerfully and Omark quickly became the world's best example of using JIT outside of Japan.

• *"At their Mesabi plant, large-size drill inventory was cut by 92%, productivity increased by 30%, scrap and rework dropped 20%, and lead time (the time it takes to go from order to finished product) was slashed from three weeks to three days.*

    •

• * *At the Oroville plant, which produces reloading equipment for firearms, inventories were reduced by 50%, lead time plummeted from six weeks to two days, and lot sizes (the number of parts produced during an individual run) were progressively cut from 500 to 30. In less than one year, some 200 products, more than 70% of the plant's entire line, were JIT.*

•

• * *At pilot operations in a log-loader plant in Prentice, Wis., total inventories were reduced by 45%, and, thanks to a new layout, parts that had once traveled 2,000 feet now move only 18 inches to get from one machine to another. Work in*

process   went   from   60   pieces   to   just   1."
https://www.inc.com/magazine/19840301/9715.html

Omark did this in the early 1980's while many American corporations are still struggling to use JIT effectively. Omark saved millions and demonstrated the power of small study groups just reading important books with the thought of learning together and getting it applied. My company, Productivity Press, sold over 35,000 copies of the Green Book in *"Janglish"*. Productivity Press later re-edited the book and put it into much better English and probably sold another 50,000 books. **I highly recommend you put all of your employees into study groups challenged to become more socially responsible and to grow the company at the same time.**

(Funny, in 1984 America had 400 certified value engineers while Toshiba had over 1600. Value Analysis/Value Engineering was invented by Larry Miles when he worked at GE.)

Dr. Shingo

17.   Make sure facilities are safe and wholesome

When younger, I was an accountant and worked in many different types of factories: woodworking, metal working, etc. and the atmosphere was horrible with dust all over, unheated, stagnant air, filthy toilets, etc. But it doesn't have to be that way. In most places, they hire cleaning people to come in, but they never did a good enough, deep enough job.

At FastCap in Ferndale, Washington, every employee cleans the factory and they even take turns cleaning the toilets, which are Toto Japanese toilets. They don't need special cleaning people and the place is spotless. (I recommend you all give yourself a great gift and buy this toilet seat. The seat is heated, and it washes your buttocks.

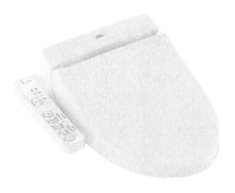

Let people do the work and take pride in the place as if it was their own. They surely spend enough time there. That is a key, ownership!

18.   Treat employees as partners and devise schemes for long-term employment

After World War II, Japanese companies were very clever when they set up life-time employment schemes. It gave people a sense of security, loyalty and allowed the company to educate and invest in them. All big companies had it and many of the smaller companies tried their best to follow.

People were carefully interviewed right out of high school, or college and keep until retirement; normally at age 60. Trained, coached, given exercise opportunities during the day, paid by age, and a high percent of earnings came from bonuses. Unions were organized by company not by industry; the employees, when dissatisfied, would wear black arm badges to protest not go out on strike to harm the company. Advancement almost always came from within. Their system allowed the company to invest in all of their employees, feeling that the investment would come back to the company. And the lifetime system worked very well, until unfortunately Japan like America was challenged by Chinese companies paying 30 cents per hour for their labor. Quickly, Japanese companies with a knee-jerk reaction switched to short term thinking, sent work to China, altered their life-time system by hiring vast numbers of part time employees and many Japanese companies are struggling to re-adjust. Just today, I read that Canon's profit was 50% lower.

Schwinn Bicycle Company was at one time highly recognized in America, ran into labor problems and went to Giant Bicycles in Taiwan to manufacture their bikes. Giant, like China today, had very low labor rates and slowly was able to do everything necessary to build the bikes and Schwinn became more of a marketer of bikes and sadly eventually went bankrupt while Giant with Schwinn's technology is a highly successful company today.

Ask yourself, *"How can you treat employees as partners and find ways for their long-term employment?"* Start with yourself. *"How would you like to see your company change?"* Write it all down and ask others to do the same thing.

19.   Everyone adheres to perfection

In 1980, I bought a Buick station wagon, my last America automobile. I remember, after buying it, I put a pad of paper on the passenger seat to write down all of the problems to be found. We just accepted the defects. American industry offered at the time a + or - 3% defect rate. You expected to find defects with the products you bought. Buick and other companies at the time offered to fix all your defects for a period of one year or 12,000 miles. We all hoped we would discover all of the major problems before the warranty period expired.

Today is different, we all want our products to be perfect.

We all should always strive for perfection in whatever we do.

I just love things well made.

Honor it, encourage it and reward it.

20.   **If you can stretch a little: challenge others to add value, to be creative so that you are being more socially responsible and not losing any money.**

Can you?

- Offer extensive time off for childcare

- Allow flextime and to work at home

- Let people make decisions based on their experience

- Pay a living wage (some companies force people onto food stamps)

- Everyone gets a retirement plan - treat all employees equally

- Everyone has a goal to align themselves with the vision of the company

- Everyone has a coach and is taught how to coach someone else

- The supervisor learns how to be a coach to bring out the best in people, to develop them, to trust them; help them fulfill the worker's potential

- Take fear out of the workplace

- Believe that all employees are good natured

- Create a good working environment where every worker can make the most of their ability

- Limit the number of rules and allow people to break them for the benefit of the customer and the company

- You want people to be enthusiastic, motivated, excited to come to work everyday

A few years back, in Portland, Oregon, I met with around 40 quality managers and I asked them, "What is your goal?" Half the people in the audience wanted "retirement."

Wow, we have to change that.

- Encourage thinking by everyone. How do you do this?

- Challenge people, compliment them, make it easier to work in the company

- Everyday praise at least five people.

When I was younger, I never remember receiving praise from my parents or my teachers. I never remember praising my wife or daughters. But, when I became a manager, I was told that it was necessary for me to praise others.

So, one day I walked into our data entry room, looked at a young woman and said, "I want to thank you for doing such an excellent job on the Budweiser project. She stopped working, turned to look at me and I felt enormous love from her. I actually felt tears coming to my eyes. I realized for the first time in my life what I was missing, not only what she was missing. Once I broke the ice, it was so easy for me to praise. Try it. You will love it.

Everyone needs a coach. There is a very inexpensive way to get one

As we wrote earlier, every great athlete has a coach and I believe that virtually every CEO has a coach, and everyone needs a coach, but the average worker does not have a coach. An inexpensive way for everyone to have a coach is to pair up people and ask them to become coaches to each other.

We want people to feel that they have the ability to achieve their goals at work and in their life. We want them to be happy. Coaches support each other to attain the sense that they can do it successfully. If they also focus on serving a higher purpose: corporate goals, missions and vision, a better society, etc. - all adds to their self-evaluation. Coaches can develop the necessary skills and learn from other great coaches.

21.   **Check lists are very powerful improvement tools.**

In America, approximately 450,000 people die from medical error. You go to a doctor or a hospital for medical assistance and there is a good chance you will be injured. Many reasons exist for these medical mistakes, but they can be substantially reduced if doctors, nurses and others were trained to use check lists.

Many years ago, I was in the hospital recovering from major surgery and Dr. Hotchkiss, head of urology at New York University Medical Center would come by each morning to examine me. On each visit, he would refer to his check list, "fourth day, remove the sutures."

158Sustaining profits and doing the right thing!

In the earlier days of aviation, flying was quite dangerous, but the industry required the use of check lists by pilots, mechanics, etc. Now flying is safer than driving.

The doctors are much too "egotistic," thinking their intelligence is adequate, but that is not true. Even a genius can forget to "tie their shoes." At the Rhode Island hospital, a few years ago, a doctor operated on the wrong side of the brain, twice, with two different people.

Everyone at work should learn to use check lists just like the pilots. Every time a mistake is made another item could be put on the check list. We want to learn how to "mistake proof," the work that we do.

Chapter VI - To have closer ties and have a deeper more positive relationship with their suppliers

Dealing fairly and ethically with our suppliers. We are dedicated to serving as good partners to the other companies, large and small, that help us meet our missions.

Most companies have a supply chain to produce products and services to satisfy their customers. Even though they are often all separate companies, they should operate seamlessly as if they were one organization producing high quality products and services. In the past, many suppliers were kept distant, even squeezed to reduce their costs. You don't want damaging shortcuts in your own company and you also should want the same for your suppliers. All the new things you will be doing to become more socially responsible, you should share and teach to your suppliers.

Your suppliers are not just vendors, they are your partners, and this partnership should be based not only on financial transactions, but also on mutual trust and loyalty. Make your suppliers feel like they are a part of your business. Inform them about your processes, such as releases of new products and promotions, and listen to their concerns.

160 Sustaining profits and doing the right thing!
1.   Set up consortiums to encourage creativity for suppliers

After a number of years when Toyota was successfully implementing Just-In-Time, (JIT), Taiichi Ohno asked their 10 top suppliers to select one skilled manager in their company to work together in a group to convert all of their companies to JIT. They did and had Dr. Shigeo Shingo meet each month with them. To me Shingo was the greatest manufacturing consultant in the 20th century. He was Ohno's teacher and also taught Industrial Engineering, problem solving techniques, to 3000 Toyota engineers.

The top 10 studied and worked as a team together. The top 10 learned from Shingo and Toyota managers and were adequately able to lead their companies to JIT. Even though suppliers had to reduce each year their costs to Toyota from 10% to 15%, they all became highly successful where most today are the world's leading suppliers of automobile parts. Toyota taught their suppliers how to reduce costs, how to implement JIT as a prime instrument to reduce costs and to become more creative and more efficient. There are very few companies like Toyota in the world that also sends their past managers to work with their suppliers to improve their productivity and quality.

One day, at Toyota Gosei, Ohno gave my study mission travelers a lecture on JIT. Afterwards, Yoshiki Iwata, Ohno's assistant at Toyota Gosei came over to me and told me he and a few others from other Toyota suppliers were leaving their companies, setting up a new company, and asked me to help introduce them to American companies. I was pleased to do it. I arranged with George Koenigsaecker, president of Jacob's Vehicle Equipment Company, a Danaher company, in Connecticut to run a Five Days and Five Nights workshop.

We attracted 45 managers at $5,000 each to attend, five additional came from *"Jake Brake,"* (a miracle for we knew nothing about it.) The event had the strange name as people worked late into the night and received very little sleep. In those five days they learned the principles of JIT, totally rearranged the plant from batch processing to flow, moved 50 machines, created total chaos but it was the most powerful training event I had ever seen. We left the plant with a lot of homework to do and they did it and became highly successful. Danaher was able to take out tons of cash as the inventory was substantially reduced and Danaher used the new process with the extra cash to buy up dozens of others manufacturing plants.   Subsequently, the name of the workshop was changed to the Kaizen Blitz.

I asked Chihiro Nakao, Nagata's partner, **"Who created JIT," Ohno or Shingo. He said, "Who came first the chicken or the egg?"** Nakao was from Taiho Kogyo, one of Toyota's top 10 suppliers. I spent one day with Nakao in Tokyo at his client and I watched him have a lot of fun teaching them JIT. He simply looked at people working and encouraged them to eliminate the wastes. I was standing near a woman working at an automated parts supply machine where she dialed in parts numbers and the machine spun around to get her the parts. Nakao asked me, *"What would Ohno say about that machine?"* I said, *"Ohno would say get rid of it."* He laughed.

I was told that Porsche was the only other company to set up these consortiums with their suppliers. Every large company should take the responsibility to work closer with their suppliers so that the gap between them disappears.

Sustaining profits and doing the right thing!

Ohno, looked at each supplier as if they were an extension, a part of Toyota, and eventually every supplier to Toyota, over 200 companies, were taught JIT.

2. Train your suppliers using your best managers, and coaches

If you set up a consortium, wonderful, if not, then set up classes to train your suppliers about your needs. Encourage them to learn Value Analysis/Value Engineering. Encourage them to run book study groups to continuously improve. You want them to deliver high quality products, on time, at the lowest possible cost.

You are learning to become socially responsible. You also want them to become socially responsible. As you learn, teach them.

3. Open up lines of communication

Once in Germany at a Sony TV plant, I noticed a large board in the receiving area and recorded were all of the problems incurred with products from another Sony plant in England. When a problem occurred, it was relayed immediately to the other plant and became visual to all.

Make sure to maintain strong and regular communication with each of your suppliers. Keep them regularly informed and up to date, on your strategy and plans so that they know where they fit in and how they can help, plan for and benefit from those plans. Make them your partner. If you appreciate their work, let them know. If something's not working for you, let them know.

4. Allow your supplier to be creative

Toyota started a process to demand reductions in costs to all of their suppliers, normally from 10% to 15% per year. They also went into the supplier to help them find ways to reduce their costs.

Ford Motor started this process, after Toyota, but Ford insisted that the supplier adhere 100% to the specifications, while Toyota wanted the part to be built by the supplier to be fully functional but allowed them to be very creative in designing and building the part. For example, the supplier could change the material or the design as long as it complied with safety, quality and functionality. While Ford wanted the reduction of the 10% but would not allow the supplier to be creative in the process.

Look, your supplier knows their product the best. Challenge them to be creative and to come up with new ideas on how to improve the value of their parts.

5. Pay them fairly

Recognize you and the supplier are on the same team. Get rid of the notion of we and they. You both have common goals. Help them succeed. Of course, you want them to give you the best most competitive pricing but help them. Don't force them to take shortcuts.

If you don't want to lose your suppliers, step one is making sure to pay them on time. If for any reason you cannot make the payment on a date agreed, then inform the supplier as soon as possible with the date on which they can expect the payment. Suppliers like timely payments just like you do.

Sustaining profits and doing the right thing!

6.   Encourage continuous improvement and reasonable cost reduction

Omark Industries mentioned earlier in this book that they made life easier for its suppliers, by sharing information so that vendors can predict more accurately their own needs and manufacturing schedules. *"Before, we worked at arm's length with suppliers, but now we want a strong marriage relationship."* - Larry White

Chapter VII - Community and Environment

"Supporting the communities in which we work. We respect the people in our communities and protect the environment by embracing sustainable practices across our businesses."

1. Invest in uplifting your community

A few years ago, I was in Tokyo and went to a Japanese Union of Scientists and Engineers (JUSE) conference where my friend Professor Noriaki Kano was presenting. While at the conference, a distinguished Indian gentleman came over to me and said, *"Norman, I want to introduce myself to you. I am Venu Srinivasan, Chairman of TVS Motor Company in India."* I said, *"TVS was my first client in India over 30 years ago."* He said, *" Yes, I was your client."* I was a little embarrassed not recognizing him.

Venu said, *"Norman, 30 years ago, I read your book The Canon Production System and it totally changed my life. It was the seed for our future success."* We spoke only for a few moments and he invited me to visit his company in Bengaluru (Bangalore), India. I said, *"I am happy to come with my wife, but you have to fly us business class."* He said, *"Fine."* I also asked him what he wanted me to teach. He said, *"Nothing. I just want you to come and look at my company."* In my entire life, that was the only time I was asked to do that. In all of the other situations, I come and teach something.

We went to Bengaluru and was met at the airport by a driver from TVS who took us to one of the world's finest hotels,

166Sustaining profits and doing the right thing!

<u>The Leela Palace.</u> It was magnificent. A very rare experience staying at such a great hotel.

The next morning the same driver picked us up and drove us to the TVS plant in Hosur, India, around 50 miles from Bengaluru.

Typical India:

The drive went through the very crowded city of almost 13 million people, pollution in the air and in the streets, cows, worshipped by the Hindus, eating from the garbage left on the side of the road; we finally reached the TVS plant, one of the finest manufacturing facilities comparable to any in the world. I had been to India over 20 times and I have never seen a plant like this one.

TVS manufactures motorcycles, sales of 2.9 billion dollars and is part of the Sundaram-Clayton, auto parts supplier, with sales over 7 billion. Venu is both chairman of TVS and Sundaram-Clayton. In 2016, Business Today magazine, with the highest circulation in India, nominated Venu as India's best CEO.

The TVS facility

A bird sanctuary outside of the plant

Spotless

Sundaram-Clayton Limited is the first company in India to win the Deming Prize in 1998. TVS Motor Company was awarded the Deming Prize in 2002. In the same year, Sundaram-Clayton was awarded the Japan Quality Medal (JQM). Next to me is Kovai, (V Kovaichelvan,) head of HR and Paul Akers. I was invited to visit TVS three times and Paul asked to travel with me on the second trip. Paul looked at me and said, *"Norman, give up sugar and wheat and lose weight."* I listened to him and lost 25 pounds.)

Venu Srinivasan - Chairman TVS

TVS became the first company in India to win the prestigious Deming Prize. Srinivasan also received a reward as the first industrialist from India for his contributions in the field of total quality management (TQM),

TVS Motor Company - Mission

"We are committed to be a highly profitable, socially responsible, and leading manufacturer of high value for money, environmentally friendly, lifetime personal transportation products under the TVS brand, for customers predominantly in Asian markets and to provide fulfillment and prosperity for employees, dealers, and suppliers."

TVS Vision Statement:

Driven by the customer

"TVS Motor will be responsive to customer requirements consonant with its core competence and profitability. TVS Motor will provide total customer satisfaction

Sustaining profits and doing the right thing!
by giving the customer the right product, at the right price, at the right time."

The Industry Leader

"TVS Motor will be one among the top two two-wheeler manufacturers in India and one among the top five two-wheeler manufacturers in Asia."

Global overview

"TVS Motor will have profitable operations overseas especially in Asian markets, capitalizing on the expertise developed in the areas of manufacturing, technology and marketing. The thrust will be to achieve a significant share for international business in the total turnover."

At the cutting edge

"TVS Motor will hone and sustain its cutting edge of technology by constant benchmarking against international leaders."

Committed to Total Quality

"TVS Motor is committed to achieving a self-reviewing organization in perpetuity by adopting TQM as a way of life. TVS Motor believes in the importance of the process. People and projects will be evaluated both by their end results and the process adopted."

The Human Factor

"TVS Motor believes that people make an organization and that its well-being is dependent on the commitment and

growth of its people. There will be a sustained effort through systematic training and planning career growth to develop employees' talents and enhance job satisfaction. **TVS Motor will create an enabling ambience where the maximum self-actualization of every employee is achieved.** *TVS Motor will support and encourage the process of self-renewal in all its employees and nurture their sense of self-worth."*

Responsible Corporate Citizen

"TVS Motor firmly believes in the integration of Safety, Health and Environmental aspects with all business activities and ensures the protection of employees and environment including development of surrounding communities. TVS Motor strives for long-term relationships of mutual trust and interdependence with its customers, employees, dealers, and suppliers."

While in India, Venu introduced me to a charity he started 21 years ago, Srinivasan Services Trust (SST), which has **uplifted 3.14 million people out of poverty.** In India, close to 650,000,000 people have no toilets and most of them do live in poverty.

There was a temple in Venu's ancestral village Srirangam, that was in need of repair. Venu invested and transformed the temple but then noticed how bad off the surrounding village was and decided to see if he could help. A few employees were brought into to work with the village people. In Indian villages the women are especially neglected, vast numbers are not educated at all. His employees went into the village where the people were living in shacks without running water, or electricity. His employees gathered around 15 women together and reviewed with them their talents and desires. The group selected skills that they could develop to earn a living. They opened a micro-bank account and pledged to contribute each week a small amount of money, even less than one dollar to teach them how to save, borrow and to run their own business.

The first example was a total success and from this SST now has 400 employees. SST works closely with the government and the community (villagers.) Most of the employees came from the villages and were trained by SST. They have worked in 5000 villages and have uplifted over 3.4 million people out of poverty. Imagine how the power of this new commitment to be socially responsible can actually benefit the entire world. If we could only get 200 companies in India to replicate what TVS has done, we could totally eliminate poverty from India

When in India, I visited 15 villages that no longer had shacks but had cement houses, running water, electricity and toilets. I also saw a factory with 15 women making chapati, Indian flat bread. They were all partners in the business drawing a salary and sharing in the profits. The factory building actually had four groups of 15 women each.

It is amazing what people can do, even those living in poverty, when someone takes the responsibility to be socially responsible.

Just imagine what your company can do similarly if the company only invested in a small group of employees. I am sure poverty in America would be drastically reduced and homelessness could be a thing of the past.

2.   Proudly growing the world's best salmon

I am blessed to be able to find and experience such greatness in our world. As with most of us, I enjoy eating great healthy food. This past year at New Seasons Market in Vancouver, Washington, I discovered New Zealand King Salmon, a little expensive, around $30 per pound but to me it is well worth it. Since I am easily susceptible to *"gout"* attacks, I do not eat meat but love to have good fish, not that easy to find. I do love the tuna *"maguro,"* found in Japan but I am often disappointed in fish bought in stores where I live.

Luckily, I discovered the New Zealand King Salmon. Normally, I am very reluctant to eat "farmed fish," with having problems like disease and pollution, impact of Biodiversity, spread of disease & antibiotic Use, sea lice, pesticide use higher Levels of omega-6 and toxic PCBs and POPs (pollutants.)

When I shop, I want to get only fresh fish.

HERALDED AS THE VERY BEST SALMON IN TERMS OF TASTE, TEXTURE AND NUTRITIONAL QUALITY

Sustaining profits and doing the right thing!

https://youtu.be/DZxf8N1abYo

Our commitment to the Ten Principles of the UN Global Compact

In 2018, we became a Participant in the United Nations Global Compact, established to drive business awareness and action in support of achieving the Sustainable Development Goals by 2030.

The Global Compact encourages participants to adopt a principles-based approach to doing business more sustainably. This means operating in ways that, at a minimum, meet fundamental responsibilities in the areas of human rights, labor, environment and anti-corruption. Our aim is to continuously incorporate the Ten Principles of the UN Global Compact into strategies, policies and procedures, fulfilling our basic responsibilities to people and planet, but also setting the stage for more detailed sustainability work in our own industry.

Ten Principles of the UN Global Compact:

Principle 1: Businesses should support and respect the protection of internationally proclaimed human rights; and

Principle 2: make sure that they are not complicit in human rights abuses.

Principle 3: Businesses should uphold the freedom of association and the effective recognition of the right to collective bargaining;

Principle 4: the elimination of all forms of forced and compulsory labor;

Principle 5: the effective abolition of child labor; and

Sustaining profits and doing the right thing!

Principle 6: the elimination of discrimination in respect of employment and occupation.

Principle 7: Businesses should support a precautionary approach to environmental challenges;

Principle 8: undertake initiatives to promote greater environmental responsibility; and

Principle 9: encourage the development and diffusion of environmentally friendly technologies.

Principle 10: Businesses should work against corruption in all its forms, including extortion and bribery.

When correctly managed, aquaculture is one of the most sustainable ways of producing animal protein.

Worldwide demand for seafood is increasing and aquaculture is a highly efficient use of the marine environment. Pressure on supplies of wild fish in the world's oceans has encouraged the development of aquaculture. In the early 1970's sea farms were established in Norway and Scotland raising Atlantic salmon. In the 1980's New Zealand followed suit with the development of sea farms raising King salmon. Aquaculture takes pressure off ocean fishing and provides the world with valuable and nutritious seafood protein.

Salmon are highly efficient to farm because they are cold blooded and virtually weightless in water.

Our success is centered on maintaining the purity of the waters in which the salmon are farmed and to keep it this way.

New Zealand King Salmon is firmly committed to sustainability and managing our resources for the long term. Given our animals are notoriously fussy about their environment, environmental integrity is at the heart of our operation. New Zealand King Salmon is dedicated to producing a top-quality product, renowned for its taste, color, and texture. So, we would not want to do anything to compromise these qualities: quality in = quality out. Quality and sustainability are achieved through managing several key factors: maintaining a clean rearing environment; ensuring healthy salmon using proactive aquaculture management; sourcing sustainable and nutritious feed ingredients; and practicing careful and humane harvesting methods.

New Zealand King Salmon has been declared a 'Best Choice' by Monterey Bay Aquarium's <u>Seafood Watch</u>.

New Zealand King Salmon is the first and only ocean-farmed salmon to have achieved the Green/'Best Choice' rating from the globally respected Seafood Watch program. This great result further supports our sustainability credentials and helps you make choices for healthy oceans. 'Best Choices' are well managed and caught or farmed in ways that cause little harm to habitats or other wildlife, and help consumers select items that are fished or farmed in ways that have less impact on the environment.

ROBUST MANAGEMENT SYSTEMS AND COMPLIANCE WITH LEGISLATION

Sustaining profits and doing the right thing!

Benthic Environmental Quality Standards and Monitoring: Daily monitoring of oxygen levels, water temperature and salinity ensures conditions are right for the salmon. The water column and the seabed are monitored by an independent science provider. Environmental conditions must be within certain standards to comply with resource consents. The environmental impact of the company's operations and processes are constantly monitored, this is to ensure the good health and productivity of the salmon, as well as making certain that the farms are not significantly affecting the surrounding water quality or the natural marine ecosystems. The ability of the environment to fully recover within several years has been demonstrated, and effective methods of monitoring and managing effects around the farms have been put in place.

Discharge: There are limits to discharge levels and we have to stick to these. It is ok to have some waste as worms and micro-organisms that live under the pens eat and break down this waste. However, tolerance levels are set, and our management systems must track this to avoid non-compliance.

BEST PRACTICE HUSBANDRY AND FARM MAINTENANCE

Cleaning: Just like land-based farming, keeping the farm clean is good for the salmon and the environment. We use high pressure net cleaners to clean our pens.

Experienced Team Members: A good understanding of environmental processes has been achieved. Our team members are highly skilled at caring for the fish and surrounding environment.

Farm Structures, Pens & Predator Nets: All structures are easily moveable and are designed to blend in as much as possible with the coastal environment. Sea pens are about 17 meters deep, and the distance to the sea floor ideally around another 15 meters, to allow plenty of current to flow through. The depth of the pens offers improved growing conditions, allowing the salmon to move below the surface water and away from surface related stress. The pens are surrounded by a large predator net, as the presence of predators - like seals, sharks and dolphins, can cause the salmon intense stress.

Feed: Feed control equipment and systems ensure efficient use of feed to minimize waste. Feed ingredients are assessed prior to inclusion in diets to avoid substances which might contaminate the environment. All feed ingredients are sourced from sustainably certified fisheries and certified GMO, BSE free and is fully traceable.

Fish Welfare: The welfare of our salmon and the health of our environment are intrinsically linked. Because of its isolation, New Zealand is uniquely free of the known pathogenic diseases that can affect salmon. Pathogens are regularly screened for by the Ministry for Primary Industries (MPI) and New Zealand King Salmon's own fish health monitoring program – none have been detected. New Zealand King Salmon fish do not suffer from sea lice as King salmon are naturally resistant and sea lice in the Southern Hemisphere are smaller than those found in the far north. Therefore, New Zealand King Salmon do not carry out any sea lice treatments.

Stocking Density: Stocking rates are kept low. 2% of the sea pen volume is salmon and 98% is sea water, which flows freely through the structures.

180Sustaining profits and doing the right thing!

Apple (AAPL) CEO Tim Cook took the stage Wednesday during the company's annual shareholders meeting to provide insight into the tech giant's performance over the past year and prospects for 2020.

And while he touched on a number of topics ranging from the ongoing coronavirus outbreak to Apple's plans to open its first store in India, one of the more interesting tidbits came when Cook addressed a question about whether Apple is working on a monitor for diabetic consumers, and if doing so would be a means for the company to see a return on its investments, or to assist its users.

"If you're a shareholder who thinks we only do things for ROI, then you're in the wrong stock," Cook told the audience at The Steve Jobs Theater in Cupertino, California.

"If you look in the health area...the research studies that you've seen in heart, hearing, women's studies, none of these have an ROI on them. They just have a cost. And we do that because we discovered early on that the way people were conducting medical research was arcane."

If it's good for the customer, it's good for the company

Apple currently offers compatibility between the iPhone and Apple Watch and glucose monitors for diabetics, but it does not have a monitor of its own. Rumors have circulated for some time about Apple working on such a feature for the Apple Watch, but those have yet to come to fruition.

While Cook said he couldn't comment on whether Apple is working on the kind of functionality that would bring glucose monitoring to its devices, he did say the company is willing to sacrifice ROI for customer satisfaction.

"Our deep belief is that if things are good for the customer, they'll eventually be good for the company," Cook said.

Of course, moves that keep Apple users happy are sure to keep them from leaving the company's ecosystem. And that means they'll eventually purchase more Apple products and devices. So, while the iPhone maker may not necessarily see any ROI on some initiatives, all roads still lead to ensuring users remain with Apple for the long haul.

And that, in the end, will still provide a return on investment.

https://tinyurl.com/tyb8dp7

Socially responsible corporations:

1. Johnson & Johnson

The company continues to seek out renewable energy options with the goal to procure 35% of their energy needs from renewable sources.

2. Google

Google is trusted not only for its environmentally friendly initiatives but also due to their outspoken CEO Sundar Pichai. Google in their data center uses 50% less energy than others in the world. They also have committed over $1 billion to renewable energy projects and enable other businesses to reduce their environmental impact through services such as Gmail

Sustaining profits and doing the right thing!

3. Ford Motor Company

Ford plans to reduce their greenhouse gas emissions using their EcoBoost engine to increase fuel efficiency. It also plans to introduce 40 electrified vehicles (electric and hybrid) by 2022, in an investment of $11 billion. According to Ford: *"We're all in on this and we're taking our mainstream vehicles, our most iconic vehicles, and we're electrifying them. If we want to be successful with electrification, we have to do it with vehicles that are already popular."*

4. Netflix

Netflix offers 52 weeks of paid parental leave, which can be taken at any time whether it is the first year of the child's life or another time that suits their needs. This compares to 18 weeks at other tech companies.

5. TOMS

TOMS mission is to donate a pair of shoes for every pair they sell and has resulted in the donation of over 60 million pairs of shoes to children in need. Profits are used to assist the visually impaired by providing prescription glasses and medical treatments, provide 'safe' drinking water and build businesses in developing countries to create jobs. They are also strong anti-bullying advocates and work with several non-governmental organizations and nonprofits to set examples of ethical behavior.

6. Bosch

Half of Bosch's research and development budget is invested in creating environmental protection technology. By 2021 the company will have invested 55.7 million to support universities and research programs that are focused on the environment, energy and mobility in Germany, India, the U.S and China through Bosch Energy Research Network, otherwise known as BERN.

7. Starbucks

With an eye to hiring, Starbucks is looking to diversify their workforce and provide opportunities for certain cohorts. By 2025 it has pledged to hire 25,000 veterans as part of their socially responsible efforts. This hiring initiative will also look to hire more younger people with the aim of "*helping jump-start careers by giving them their first job*'. While globally the company has joined with the UN Refugee Agency to scale up the company's support and efforts to reach refugee candidates to hire 10,000 refugees by 2022.

8. The Walt Disney Company

Disney is committed to reducing their carbon footprint with goals for zero net greenhouse gas emissions, zero-waste, and a commitment to conserve water. They are actively ensuring that they set strict international labor policies to protect the safety and rights of their employees.

They are also active in the community and encourage employees to do the same. They also have healthy living initiatives to promote healthy eating habits amongst employees.

9. Lego

Lego will invest $150 million over the next 15 years with a focus on addressing climate change and reducing waste. It has reduced their packaging as well as investing in an alternative energy source and plans to source 100% renewable energy by 2020. To accomplish this the company will hire a team to support its commitment to using sustainable materials and plans to reach a 90% recycling rate.

https://cutt.ly/Ctq33eL

Look around your area and see what you can do to help your community.

2.   Make the company buildings and the surrounding environmentally beautiful

Once I visited an Asahi Beer factory and was totally amazed. When younger I was not a beer drinker at all. I just didn't like the *"sour,"* taste, but Asahi came along and came out with their Asahi Dry Beer which took away that bitterness, so I was very happy to visit the plant.

3. Send trainers and managers to teach at the local schools

The US now ranks 27th in the world for its levels of healthcare and education, according to a new study and the latest findings from the Pew Research Center have the US in 38th place out of 71 countries when it comes to math scores and 24th place when it comes to science. In 1990, the US ranked sixth in the world for its levels of education and health — 21 spots ahead of where it is now.

Shocking. The new corporate commitment to become socially responsible is vitally needed to help our society.

Our primary school system has traditionally been educating children to fit industry's needs, but it has done a terrible job. Yes, our factories went from high skilled to repetitive and boring work which required very little education, but much of that work has gone to China and other low-cost countries. Our educational system needs help and corporate America must now step in.

Corporations are very influential in their local communities and must now take a greater role in educating our youth. I am sure you can do it. You just have to embrace your community's well-being as you do your corporation's well-being.

4. Set up training facilities to train the youth skills to become masters

As mentioned earlier, Germany and other European countries have training systems to educate children to learn mechanical and electronic skills. We must go back and do it. We have no time to waste.

Set up a plan now with your communities.

Sustaining profits and doing the right thing!

5. Invest in keeping the cities near your facilities clean

Researchers at Yale and Columbia ranked countries' environmental performance based on 25 metrics, including water and air quality, habitat protection and the impact of the environment on the health of the population. European countries make up more than half of the top 30, while the U.S. ranks 61st.

As I mentioned, I have visited Japan 93 times, mostly to find new management books. Japan is an exceptionally clean country. You rarely ever see people through garbage from their cars. But, one of the reasons the streets are very clean is that Japan pays elder people to go out and pick things up.

Many years ago, I worked with Chuck who would laugh and just throw things outside the car window and say, *"I am giving work for the street cleaners."* We have to change that attitude. Wouldn't it be great to include in your corporate advertising items to support your new commitment to be more socially responsible? People buy what you advertise.

6. Help eliminate the homeless problem

Once again, our government is helpless to change the current problem. There were an estimated 37,878 homeless veterans estimated in the United States (shame on us,) and a total of 558,230 homeless. We are not the worst in the world, but I am sure industry can find solutions.

7. Eliminate pollution

Around 20 years ago, I was in New Delhi, the capital of India, walking in the streets. I thought I was in a burning building. I immediately got air tickets to get out.

Years ago, I went through a tanning factory in West Virginia which had the worst air quality imaginable. I don't know how human beings could work there. And the highly polluted water just poured into a pond.

Another time I was standing in the street in Japan and a truck with hogs went by and was probably the worst smell of my entire life.

These extremes of pollution come from industry. I know we have improved but we still have a long way to go.

8. Reduce harmful wastes that hurt the environment

This new commitment is to be socially responsible - to help create a better world for us and for our children to live in. The door is now open, and we are moving in a wonderful direction.

You should not wait for the government to tell you what to do. You know what is right. Plastics is a problem to be solved right now. For example, there is new plastic material that is biodegradable. We just have to make the necessary changes now.

Ohno came up with his seven wastes to solve Toyota's problems to get to Just-in-time; other companies might have similar problems, but everyone should carefully define their own wastes and not just copy Ohno's. Funny even hospitals with Lean programs are attacking Ohno's wastes when

188Sustaining profits and doing the right thing!

hospitals main problems are totally different: 450,000 people are dying of medical error, 70,000 are dying each year of drug overdose, 50% of doctors are going through burnout, and the State of Oregon gets 100,000 calls a year about child abuse. We should identify our own strategic problems and then come up with the wastes to address them.

Here though we are looking at pollution and the other physical, environmental wastes that are destroying the earth and eventually everything that is living. Of course, governments should be the prime group to address this issue, but they are not doing it well enough. I wish we could change the very structure of governments but that is just a *"pipe dream."* Industry must rise to the occasion and save the world. And I believe that industry is one of the prime creators of the world's pollution.

Let us look at some of these wastes and see what you are capable of doing.

Municipal solid wastes - industry has a lot of power /er local governments. Get involved in your local government ιd demand that something positive happens.

Agricultural and animal waste - our food supply keeps ; alive and is killing us at the same time. The world's 1.5 llion cows and billions of other grazing animals emit dozens polluting gases, including lots of methane. Two-thirds of all nmonia comes from cows. Cows emit a massive amount of ethane through belching, with a lesser amount through ιtulence.

Medical wastes - Obesity and many other health issues should be looked at with fresh eyes. A study from the National Center for Health Statistics at the Centers for Disease Control and Preventions (CDC) showed that 39.6%

of US adults age 20 and older were obese (37.9% for men
and 41.1% for women).

Figure 1. Prevalence of obesity among adults aged 20 and
over, by sex and age: United States, 2015–2016

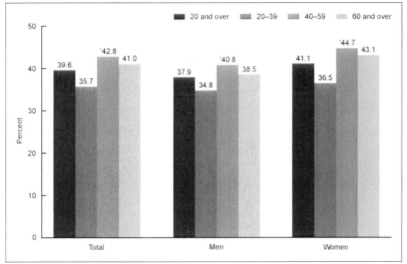

SOURCE: NCHS, National Health and Nutrition Examination
Survey, 2015–2016

Last year, I visited my doctor and in the reception
area, five people, all obese, two in wheelchairs. I asked my
doctor, *"Why don't you help them lose weight."* She said,
"They are all addicted." Yes, we know that but surely our
medical community must be able to help. And look what
obesity and employee's health is costing your company. Do
something about it. Put them into self-group therapy
sessions. Have them read and discuss together ways to live
healthier. Let's get MacDonald and all the other fast food
chains to start to serve healthy food. Being socially
responsible is a challenge to help your organization, your
community and the world.

Sustaining profits and doing the right thing!

Obesity is a prime cause of many health ailments and your organizations are financial responsible. In 2017, U.S. health care costs were $3.5 trillion. That makes health care one of the country's largest industries. It equals 17.9% of gross domestic product. In comparison, health care cost $27.2 billion in 1960, just 5% of GDP. Average health care per-person is nearly $10,000 on average. A good percentage of this cost is paid by American organizations.

What can you do to help reduce medical wastes, expenses?

1. Educate your associates.
2. Have a contest and offer rewards to those who stay healthy - Toyota would put your name into a barrel, if you did not miss one day of work, and once a year give 10 free automobiles.
3. Set up a committee to search for ways to reduce your medical expenses

Other wastes to address:

- Radioactive **waste -**
- Hazardous **waste -**
- Industrial non-hazardous **waste -**
- Construction and demolition debris -
- Extraction and mining **waste -**
- Oil and gas production **waste -**
- Fossil fuel combustion **waste -**

Chapter V - Generating long-term value for shareholders, who provide the capital that allows companies to invest, grow and innovate. We are committed to transparency and effective engagement with shareholders.

As you progress towards being more socially responsible you are faced with a number of challenges:

1.   Can you invest in improving customer service, employee development, supplier relations and the community/environment and also sustain your current profits?

2.   Are you able and willing to sacrifice short-term profits for long-term benefits?

You have to decide. Believe strongly that by adding value, you will be able to sustain and improve profits.

ATT Bell Labs at one time was probably America's most innovative organization. ATT discovered that it could lower its costs by creating innovative phone equipment. From this it followed that it could increase its income faster by assisting its suppliers by providing them with better technology, even if it gave away the technology to its suppliers. Bell Labs was referred to as *"The Idea Factory"* or *"The Crown Jewel,"* arguably the leading research organization in Information Technology and Communications. Nine of their associates were awarded the Nobel Prize and their associates created/invented:

- The two-way radio
- Proximity fuses
- Semiconductor devices
- Radar
- Computers
- The "bazooka"
- First encrypted communications systems
- Gas laser
- Super conductivity
- Background radiation
- C++ programming language
- Unix
- Etc. etc. etc.

To innovate, Bell labs required the smartest people— and it needed a lot of them, so as to foster explosive ideas. ... Bell Labs needed to house its critical mass of scientists and engineers close to one another so they could exchange ideas; it also needed to give them all the tools they needed. At one time Bell Labs had about 4,000 scientists and engineers.

In 1984, ATT broke up into smaller telephone companies and in 1996 Bell Labs unfortunately was spun off to Lucent Technologies now owned by Nokia.

You must find ways to reconstruct the idea of Bell Labs in your company.

Continue to pursue profits but with the long-term in view

194 Sustaining profits and doing the right thing!

Appendix

In the Appendix are material and interviews from some of the world's most successful business leaders, writers and consultants.

1.   Konosuke Matsushita, started and was the former CEO of Matsushita Electric, Panasonic, one of the largest companies in Japan.

"Follow the Laws of Nature

Obey the laws of nature: This is the very core of Matsushita Konosuke's business philosophy. Successful business is ordinary, normal business, selling at a price that allows a fair margin or profit, collecting payment on time, and so on. In setting the price of a product, for example, one has to seek a natural balance between the profit due the manufacturer and the capacity of the customer to pay. If a product cost $1 to manufacture; it ought to be sold for $1.10. Selling under cost as an advertising gimmick, for example, or at an excessively high price in hopes of making a quick profit, constitute bad business. Clever strategies and careful calculations may be important, but simple universal laws must always be observed.

Put Up an Umbrella When it Rains

When asked the secret of successful management, Matsushita Konosuke would often reply with a question of his own: 'What would you do if you got caught in the rain?' Invariably, the answer would be 'Open an Umbrella.' The point was that you do what common sense dictates. You sell at a price that makes a profit; you make sure you collect the proceeds of the sales; and when your products don't

Sustaining profits and doing the right thing!

sell well, don't try to force sales by manipulating prices or quality. If there is a formula for business success, he felt, it is operating in this straightforward, down-to-earth way, as simply and sensibly as opening an umbrella in the rain. When it comes to business, however, a surprising number of people let selfish motives override their common sense and they wind up wandering around unprotected in the rain.

A Leader Should Have Vision

Leaders in any field, Matsushita thought, should always have a clear vision of what they want to do, and only then approach others for support or opinions. 'Simply acting on the advice of others without any ideas of your own,' he said, 'is not leadership.' Seeking the input of others is very important, of course, but only if the leader maintains a firm sense of authority and ultimate control. A leader who serves as a firmly fixed axis can most effectively mobilize others and maximize the results of what they do.

The Public is Right

Because effective decision making is one of the most crucial aspects of business management, all managers worry about what yardstick to base their decisions on. For Matsushita Konosuke, the most secure foundation for decision making lay in prevailing public opinion. Of course, he knew that the majority was not always right, as history has repeatedly shown. But in the long run, he felt society has an almost transcendent sense of good judgement. As has been wisely observed, you can fool all of the people some of the time, and some of the people all of the time, but not all of the people all of the time.

A few years after starting Matsushita Electric, a tax official came to investigate the accounts of the rapidly prospering company. The official presented his case to Matsushita Konosuke arguing that the company's profit was greater than what had been declared in its tax statement. After a couple of sleepless nights mulling over the matter, Matsushita concluded that, ultimately, the money did belong to the country. The next day, he promptly told the tax collector to collect whatever amount was outstanding, and the investigation came simply and smoothly to a close. Later Matsushita realized that a company which pools massive amounts of capital, takes up great tracts of land, and employs many people is, though ostensibly a private enterprise, fundamentally a public institution. It was this line of thinking that led him to the further conviction that an enterprise is beholden to society, making it even a kind of crime to run a deficit.

You Have to Like Your Job

The crucial difference between a successful businessman and a poor one is that the former loves the work of business management and the latter does not. It has long been said that 'What you enjoy, you do well' and Matsushita Konosuke made this rule his guide. If you like your work to the point that you think it is your natural calling, you'll be innovative and flexible, confident in making decisions and acting on them, and successful as you move toward your goals. If, on the other hand, you think management is a worthwhile occupation but are only in the job for wanting something better to do, or inspire you, and it will be difficult for you ever to become confident and successful in your work.

Sustaining profits and doing the right thing!
Dreams Should be Shared

As president of Matsushita Electric, Matsushita Konosuke took every opportunity to inform his employees of his plans and dreams for the company's future. These included the Five-Year Plan announced in 1956 aimed at quadrupling sales and the project begun in 1960 to institute the five-day workweek by 1965. Most companies at the time were afraid to publicize such plans-to show their cards, as it were-for fear of the information leaking out and being taken advantage of by competitors. Fully aware of what the consequences might be, Matsushita Konosuke chose to keep his employees well-informed, because he wanted them to share in his dreams for the company, and because he believed it was simply the proper thing for the proprietor of a business to do. Matsushita Konosuke became known as the manager who talked about his dreams,' and it was those dreams that directed and inspired the people who worked for him.

Provide Direction and Moral Support

Looking back over his career later in life, Matsushita Konosuke recalled how he had been ill quite a bit of the time and had been forced to leave the actual running of the company to his staff, providing advice, encouragement, and support from his sick bed. After the end of World War II, the fundamental equality of a company president and his employees as human beings became established with the spread of democratic values. Matsushita changed his approach to personnel management to reflect that equality: when handling down an order, he did so in the spirit of a polite request rather than a command. The product of this approach was a feeling of respect and gratitude for the labors of the employees, that might be expressed by saying

'That was a good job well done!' and offering a cup of tea or other refreshment after a successful accomplishment. A president could not just sit passively by while his staff toiled, moreover; he had to carefully guide the company according to sound business principles and with a strong sense of mission. Although Matsushita could hardly go around offering such personal gestures and words of thanks to each member of his staff, the idea of a company president as the compass for the enterprise and the 'server of tea' was at the root of Matsushita's view of the role of top management.

Stick to Fair Prices

In the days when Matsushita Electric was just a small local workshop, Matsushita Konosuke would go out to sell its products himself. Some of his customers would press him to lower his prices, but in the face of their persistent requests, he would recall the faces of his young workers sweating in the factory in the summer heat, and he would hold his ground, zealously defending his prices by saying: 'Our prices are based on normal calculations taking into account the products themselves and the efforts of the people who have toiled to produce them. Cutting these prices would be as painful as cutting my own flesh.' Lowering prices under pressure from customers, he felt, was bad business practice. Matsushita Electric has always endeavored to set prices in accordance with what society at large considered fair and reasonable.

Business is Do-or-Die

Matsushita Konosuke would not tolerate the notion that business was a matter of timing or good fortune. 'Business,' he would say, 'is not a matter of the luck-of-the-

draw; it is a sword fight. In a real sword fight, one slip-up and you've lost your head. It's the same in business. Certainly, these are times when you win a little and times when you lose a little, but to think that you can succeed by persisting in a one-step-forward-one-step-back approach is fundamentally mistaken. Business does not go badly because of timing, luck or any other external factor. You must always see problems as arising from some fault within your own style of management.' Like the samurai, who carried swords to be used when their life was on the line, Matsushita believed a businessman's total responsibility for his actions on the job.

Products are the Progeny of Labor

In addition to his extraordinary passion for manufacturing, Matsushita Konosuke kept track of the products his company made after they were sold. 'The goods we make here every day,' he would tell his employees, 'are like children we raise with tender care. Selling them is like seeing those children grow up and go out into the world. It is only natural, then, that we should be concerned about how they are getting on in their lives, and so go and see for ourselves.' He believed that maintaining this concern for what you produce is the first step toward building an ordinary supplier-client relationship into a stronger link based on mutual trust.

Complaints Strengthen Bonds

Most of us would rather receive a compliment than a complaint or have merits rather than faults pointed out, but in business Matsushita Konosuke saw things differently. 'Naturally I'm delighted when a buyer expresses compliments,' he would say, 'but I'm just as pleased to get a letter of complaint.' His reasoning was that if customers didn't bother to complain, that meant they had already decided not to buy any more products from your company. If, on the other hand, they expressed their dissatisfaction, even to the point of seriously considering going elsewhere for their needs, they were still interested. As long as you are sincere, treat their complaint with respect, and root out the cause of the problem, in the end it is your good faith they will remember. The relationship will be that much stronger for it. Far from being an attack, therefore, a complaint should be treated as a valuable opportunity to strengthen ties.

Transparent Management Fosters Growth

Managers, especially sole proprietors, all too often treat company assets like their own personal possessions. Matsushita Konosuke made a point of separating his personal accounts from those of the company even when he had no more than 10 employees working for him. As the company grew larger, he made it a regular monthly practice to announce the details of the company's accounts for all employees, from the top executive to the lowest apprentice, to see for themselves. 'starting that practice', he reflected years later, 'made the atmosphere in the workshop much brighter. Seeing their efforts directly reflected in figures before their eyes seemed to afford a sense of satisfaction and purpose in their work.' Needless to say, this sense of satisfaction was directly linked to the company's subsequent growth. Matsushita, therefore, came to believe that openness in management practice is crucial to a business that seeks to grow.

Dam Management

Sustaining profits and doing the right thing!

In theory, an enterprise has to be growing at a healthy, steady pace at all times; but in reality, various economic factors can inhibit such growth. Matsushita Konosuke believed, however, that continued progress is possible with the right approach, such as by employing what he called the 'dam method' of management.

By damming a river, you can store enough water to have a constant supply regardless of the vicissitudes of the seasons or the weather. Likewise, in business, you should maintain a suitable surplus of resources in all areas – equipment, capital, planning, and product development – based on a prudent assessment of your future needs in each. This kind of oversupply might at first seem wasteful, but in the long run it is a crucial form of insurance for stable development

Bad Times have Their Bright Side

Most businessmen are happy as long as the economy is growing, but when recession sets in, they grumble. Matsushita Konosuke had an idiosyncratic view of the meaning of good times. During prosperous times, he would say, 'you move along at a gallop; in times of recession, you saunter at a leisurely pace. When you're galloping, you haven't got time to look around you, so you don't notice any problem. But when your pace slackens, you can see everything in all directions, and if you notice something wrong you have time to fit it.' In other words, even a slump has its merits. When sales are down because of a sluggish market, you can attend to after-sales service more thoroughly than you could before, or perhaps put more effort into training personnel. If you are willing to make this kind of effort during the bad times, even a recession becomes a rare and welcome opportunity.

People are Diamonds in the Rough

Poor health prevented Matsushita Konosuke from playing the role of active executive leader of his business. He had little choice but to entrust the day-to-day operations to his subordinates. His company started out as a small, unknown workshop, hardly the kind of organization to attract outstanding talent. So, Matsushita put immense effort into personnel training and development. 'However, much you rub it,' he reflected later, 'you can't make a diamond from an ordinary stone. But if you have a diamond in the rough, you can draw out its gleam with careful polishing. And depending on how you polish it and cut it, you can make it sparkle and shine in various different ways. People are just like uncut diamonds; they each have the potential for various kinds of brilliance, qualities which, if polished right, will shine radiantly. It is very important for personnel managers to have a proper grasp of this concept, and to attempt to draw out the special strengths of each employee.' Understanding the great potential of human nature is at the heart of successful development of human resources.

People before Products

Right from the very early days of the company, Matsushita Konosuke would often instruct his employees thus: 'If someone asks you what Matsushita Electric produces, tell them we produce people, and only then mention that we also produce electrical goods.' He always believed that the measure of a company was the people who worked for it, that no enterprise could succeed if its

Sustaining profits and doing the right thing!

employees did not grow as human beings, and that business, first and foremost, was about cultivating human potential. No matter how much capital, technology or equipment an enterprise boasts, it is bound to fail if its human resources are not developed. And Matsushita did not mean merely improving employees' technical know-how or sales skills, though these are certainly part of the concept. For him, the true aim of personnel development was to cultivate individual self-reliance and responsibility, to guide employees to an understanding of the value and significance of their own work and of the obligation of the company to contribute to society. To make them, in other words, productive, conscientious members of their industry and their society.

Trust your Employee

One of Matsushita Konosuke's basic tenets was trust. The first products of Matsushita Electric were electric sockets molded from insulation material. At the time, the knowledge of ingredients of this insulation was an industrial secret. Lest competition grow intense by letting such crucial technology leak out, the owners of most factories kept the formula for insulation a closely guarded secret confided only to family members or trusted colleagues. Once he and his co-workers discovered the way to make insulation, however, Matsushita shared it with all the people in his employ, down to the newest shop-boy. He reasoned that keeping things secret meant extra unnecessary worry, was troublesome on the practical level, and above all inefficient. While some of his fellow manufacturers warned him the dangers of betrayal, he eventually discovered that, on the contrary, the morale and loyalty of his employees soared when they were entrusted with vital information and important tasks to perform. This experience convinced

Matsushita that people rise to a task only if you trust them, and that even on the rare occasions when your trust is betrayed, it is best to just let it pass. Matsushita was widely known as one who completely trusted his employees, leaving them to carry out tasks with complete confidence in their abilities and judgement.

Subordinates can be your Superiors

Matsushita Konosuke was often called the 'God of Management' for his skill not only in business but also in handling people. Matsushita insisted there was no special secret to his success, that he simply did the obvious thing in the usual way. If something was peculiar to his approach, it could be revealed by his remark that 'To me, my subordinates have always seemed so much better than myself. In my eyes they are all quite impressive, without exception better educated and more talented than I am.' As company president there were times when he had to reproach an employee, but he confided that he would be thinking as he did so how that person was superior to him in various ways. For Matsushita Konosuke, who started out without adequate education and suffered chronic illness, this humility was one of the cornerstones of a successful philosophy of personnel management.

Focus on Strengths

There are two types of people: those who concentrate on other people's weaknesses and those who pay most attention to their strengths. Matsushita Konosuke used to say that, as a manager, focusing on people's shortcomings quickly gave him a headache. When you only look at weaknesses, every person you encounter appears inadequate in one way or another, and you end up

Sustaining profits and doing the right thing!

vacillating about assigning anyone to the job or task you have at hand. Subordinates, too, are bound to be unhappy if all you ever notice is their failings. 'I always tried Matsushita said, to notice people's strong points seven times out of 10 and their weaknesses the remaining three.' By paying more attention to employees' strengths, he believed, he would be more likely to think of ways to put those strengths to good use. The important thing is to keep your assessment of others' strengths and weaknesses in proper proportion.

Keep a Firm Grip on Loose Reins

When it came to assigning jobs, Matsushita Konosuke focused on his employees' strong points. Even if a person might not have much experience or distinguished record of performance, if he seemed to have the aptitude for the job, Matsushita was ready to entrust it fully to him. This approach fostered an abundance of experienced and reliable personnel at Matsushita Electric. One of the reasons behind this approach was Matsushita's own poor health, which, right from the start of his business, forced him to rely heavily on others in the day-to-day operation of the company. But though he easily delegated work and authority to others, he did not thereby abdicate responsibility for what was going on under him. He expected to receive reports about particular projects at appropriate intervals, and he would interject further orders or advice when he thought necessary. That was the duty of a person in a position of responsibility, he believed. Forced by chronic bronchial illness to rest for extended periods, Matsushita quite often summoned his subordinates to his bedside to report on the business, in response to which he would give new instructions or offer help in problems they were encountering. He called this keeping "a firm grip on loose reins"; it was Matsushita way of distributing authority and nurturing the talents of his staff.

Be Realistic about People

When the staff of Matsushita Electric had grown to about 80, it came to Matsushita Konosuke's attention that one of his employees had committed a financial indiscretion. Being a person with a deep aversion to the corrupt or unclean, Matsushita worried considerably about how he should deal with the matter, to the point it kept him awake at night. Then he thought to himself: 'I wonder how many people there are in Japan whom society calls criminals. If we include all those who have committed only minor misdemeanors, there must be about a million. If that's what it's like on the national scale, it's hardly surprising that a company of 80 people should have at least one dishonest employee. It's asking too much to expect that everyone we employ will be totally upright and virtuous. If I can't accept that some will succumb to temptation, I won't be able to use people to their full potential.' With that realization, his anxieties vanished, and his personnel policies thereafter became more aggressive.

An Employee Is a 'Client'

With the wave of democracy that swept Japan after the war, labor unions were formed throughout industry, and at Matsushita Electric, too, there were union marches and rallies to press various worker demands. Watching these demonstrations, Matsushita Konosuke was reminded of the old saying that 'to employ people is to employ trouble.' But at the same time,' he reflected, 'Taking people into one's employ can be trying, but looked at from a different angle, all these people are like clients, I must treat them with the utmost care. Clients generally expect too much, but if you want to do business with them, you don't think of it as too much; you thank them for their patronage and do what you can to keep it.' Reasoning in this way, he not only eased his anxiety over the difficulties of working with the labor union, but even decided to avoid thinking in terms of labor versus management. He preferred to deal with his staff and employees as co-workers, in fact, as people whom he served. In the end, it was the truth of another proverb that he fell back on: Soliciting the service of others is the same as serving them.

Consulting is Better than Ordering

When as company president, Matsushita Konosuke had orders to give a subordinate, he was known for broaching the topic as if seeking advice or offering a suggestion. In other words, instead of simply saying 'Would you do such-and-such,' he would say something like 'I've been thinking we could do such-and-such this way; what do you think?' or 'Would you undertake this job?' thus making this subordinates feel free to present their own opinions and suggestions on the matter. The result of this approach was that his staff would undertake assignments as if on their own initiative. People display their best abilities, he found, when they are working on their own volition and responsibility. Matsushita's style of personnel management and training was grounded in his firm grasp of these subtleties of human nature.

Don't Imagine 'Impossible'

Henry Ford once remarked that the smarter the engineer the more likely he was to say that something couldn't be done. Matsushita had a similar idea about the connection between knowledge and innovation: 'We speak of the shortcomings of the purely intellectual approach, but this refers to our wariness of half-baked theories that can prevent us from proceeding to a practical solution. If necessity is the mother of invention, then simple, unaffected determination is its father. Even when everyone around you say it's impossible, if you step back and rethink your task in the simplest possible terms, free of the noise of over-erudite and preconceived notions, often the solutions will come to you, out of the blue, so to speak.' For this reason, Matsushita's own lack of formal education was a blessing in disguise, allowing him to see to the heart of problems free of the constraints of academic or unsubstantiated ideas.

Small Companies have the Advantage

'The bigger the organization,' Matsushita Konosuke believed, 'the harder to improve its efficiency. The organization where efficiency is the most difficult to improve is the government. It's not that public servants don't work hard; it's that the environment they are part of prevents them from working hard. Surrounded by conditions that obstruct their efforts, they fall into an attitude of passivism.' Large companies, he felt, have the same problem. Small enterprises would soon be out of business if pessimism set in, and there is much more freedom of initiative and activity. Companies with 20 to 50 employees enjoy a responsive, personalized environment in which it is easy for each person to understand the personalities as well as the work being done by the others. Matsushita felt that such companies could attain 120 percent performance from their employees.

Start on a Clean Slate

Sometime in the early 1960s, when Japan was being pressured to open up its markets, a certain Japanese auto manufacturer asked Matsushita Electric to lower its prices for *car radios by 20 percent, saying it was necessary to cope with increased foreign competition. At first glance this seemed a thoroughly unreasonable request, but for the sake of the Japanese automotive industry, Matsushita Konosuke decided he must do his best to lower the price. The problem was that a 20-percent price cut on a product that until then had been making only a three-percent profit would put the company way in the red. At that point, Matsushita directed his engineers to go back to the drawing board and completely rethink the design until they came up with a product that satisfied the customer's needs and still cleared a reasonable profit for the company. In a few months, they filled his order. When circumstances call for changes, it is usually better to go back to the drawing board rather than trying to retouch something you have already produced.*

Management is Perpetual Creation

For Matsushita Konosuke, business was a creative activity on a par with the fine arts; it was a process of producing something valuable out of nothing. You start with an idea for an enterprise. Then you hammer out a basic plan, raise the necessary capital, and put together the necessary facilities and equipment. Finally, you hire employees, develop a line of products (or services), manufacture (or provide) them, thereby making a contribution to society. Moreover, each area of management has its own mode of operation, and anyone hoping to succeed in business must be able to adapt those modes quickly to the constantly changing social and economic milieu. In this respect, management diverges from other creative endeavors, since while a painter can call a painting finished and put down his brush, the work of a person in business is never complete. In this sense, business management is an organic, living art form.

In his address at the management policy meeting in January 1946, only months after the war ended, Matsushita Konosuke called on his employees to let the long road of Japanese industrial reconstruction begin, as it were, right there at Matsushita Electric. As a first step, he wanted the management to set an example of diligence and industry for the rest of the employees. For his own part, he made a New Year resolution never to be late for work and not to take off one working day. But then, on the very first working day after the New Year holiday, the car that was to meet him at Osaka Station wasn't there when he arrived, and he was 10 minutes late for work. When Matsushita asked the driver why he was delayed, he said it was his own carelessness, rather than circumstances beyond his control. Matsushita ordered a reduction on one month's salary for the driver and the driver's supervisor, and a one-month wage cut for himself, since he was responsible for both of these employees. He then promptly reported the matter to the entire staff at the morning staff meeting. Matsushita Konosuke firmly believed in rewarding those who performed meritorious service and punishing those who were negligent, beginning with himself.

Attention to the Job

One piece of advice Matsushita Konosuke gave to his employees in the early days of the company was: You may be a well-educated, clever and virtuous person, but those qualities will not necessarily make you a successful businessman. In addition, you must acquire the knack for business. Asked how this is done, he would reply thus: 'By giving your best to each and every task you take on, and by reflecting on your performance with an honest and unprejudiced eye. If you do this constantly, day after day,

212Sustaining profits and doing the right thing!

eventually you will be able to do your job unerringly.' The point was that you cannot study how to be successful; you acquire the secret to business success gradually by applying yourself with conscious effort from day to day." Permission received from PHP Institute, Inc.: Konosuke Matsushita *"His Life and His Legacy"*

The seven principles of the Matsushita Way:

1. Contribution to society
2. Fairness and Honesty
3. Cooperation and Team Spirit
4. Untiring Effort for Improvement
5. Courtesy and Humility
6. Adaptability
7. Gratitude

85 Key Point

The above seven principles will be clearly understood, and tips of how to implement the principles will be enumerated in the following 85 points, grouped into eight components of leadership and management:

Responsibility

1. The chain of responsibility begins at the top.
2. Responsibility and remuneration are in proportionate ratio.
3. Taking responsibility for failures - paves the path to success.
4. Responsibility and "courageous worrying".
5. Responsibility and sincerity.
6. The responsibility to motivate.
7. The responsibility to communicate.
8. The responsibility to lead.
9. Responsibility and influence on politics.

Decision Making

10. The significance of decision-making.
11. Decision-making and the onus of responsibility
12. Leadership and decision-making.
13. Technology vs. Insight in decision-making.
14. The role of feedback in decision-making.
15. The right decisions...at the right time.
16. Common Sense.
17. The essential and the inessential.
18. The importance of an unbiased mind.
19. The decision to retreat is as crucial as the decision to proceed (calling a spade a spade).
20. Courage and ethics in decision-making.

What it takes to be Successful

21. Recognizing YOUR weaknesses – is the first step to success.

Motivation

Resources

42. Just "doing your job" is not enough.

43. Good managers are like ballet dancers... always on their toes.

44. Let your workers face their own challenges.

45. Delegate without delegating all.

46. Square pegs in round holes.

47. Opening Doors – all owning opportunities for growth.

Teamwork

48. The ocean of collective wisdom.

49. A wise manager seeks the counsel of many.

50. A chain is only as strong as each link that constitutes it. 51. Not yours or mine, but ours the transparent glass policy. 52. Encouraging Initiative.

53. The pros and cons of hierarchy.

54. The world is your oyster.

55. An open mind is more valuable than a fancy R&D outfit.

Ups and Downs

56. Oranges and Lemons

57. Stand behind your people, and your people will stand behind you.

58. Make the most of the bad times.

59. The University of Adversity.

60. Tough times call for time out.

61. When the going gets tough, the tough get going.

62. Never lose the strength of your convictions.

63. Count your blessing.

Sustaining profits and doing the right thing!

Energy, Will and Drive

From: http://www.successcorners.com
Vijay Michihito Batra

Chapter VIII - Additions

John M. Bernard, author of Government That Works, Business at the Speed of Now: Fire Up Your People, Thrill Your Customers, and Crush Your Competitors and is a consultant to state governors.

The following is a guide to help you be a more effective leader:

What does the leader do?

1. Stops solving routine problems where he does not have the most direct problem knowledge

2. Quits jumping into solutions and insists the facts about the problem are understood

3. Acknowledges he / she is a learner, too, and is trying to figure out the best way to do things

4. Speaks honestly about what he is thinking directly to the person he is thinking about

5. Works to provide value to others as a leader, taking initiative to address situations by providing what is needed to serve customers and coworkers

Sustaining profits and doing the right thing!

> 6.   Strives to be consistent and act with integrity in every situation
>
> 7.   Consciously identifies and removes obstacles to what he and the business are trying to accomplish
>
> 8.   Communicates clearly and strongly his commitment to make the changes necessary to achieve the company's mission, vision, values and key goals

What does that set-in motion?

> 1.   Causes people to start taking responsibility to solve their own problems
>
> 2.   People slow down solving problems on pure Intuition, they seek to understand what the problem might be underneath instead of what is on top
>
> 3.   Makes it OK for people to admit they are lost, struggling, confused
>
> 4.   Candid conversations, shared understanding, openness and honesty. Going directly to the person who you have an issue with and addressing it head on
>
> 5.   Draws attention to situations that represent constraints or opportunities in a way that engages others in creating solutions that benefit the whole

6.   People and an organization that is consistent and keeps its word.

7.   Reliability and trust permeate the air and people know that everything is done with integrity

8.   Openly exposing the obstacles and driving decisive action, rather than pretending they did not exist or simply failing to see them

9.   Belief that the mission, vision, values and key goals are dead serious not just talk

What does that eventually cause?

1.   Moves responsibility for solving problems to the lowest possible level

2.   Problems get solved because they are understood; solutions focus on the root cause not symptoms.

3.   Fractures the notion of hierarchy based on position authority

4.   Problems get addressed because people stop walking around them. Honesty and candor become valued and practiced. Deep, trusting relationships are built

5.   The organization learns to take initiative in addressing situations that provide benefit and develops leaders that make things happen that otherwise would not have occurred

6.   High integrity, loyalty, repeat business, and long-term employees. Obstacles & opportunities are out in the open & easy to put on the table.

7.   Problems get solved and strategies deliver the expected results; excuses for failure are eliminated

8.   People who are resistant to the changes realize this is not a safe position to be in. They either leave or figure out how to get on board the changes

Without this we:

1.   Jump to solutions, and everyone has their opinion which will work. Often the most vocal person wins or the person who is most willing to take on the project

2.   Jump into solutions, and make assumptions about the root cause that are not based in fact. Our solution does not solve the problem

3.   Stick to the hierarchical model acting as those the more senior you are the righter answers you have

4.   Walk around the people issues and sacrifice what matters out of a shear unwillingness to address the real issues

5.   Remain stuck in the status quo with the attitude that circumstances are to blame for the current reality

6.   We hide problems that cause inconsistent performance, missed deadlines, blaming for failures and shortcomings, and financially struggle.

7.   We plow resources into something that will not be successful, because no one is either willing or able to remove the obstacles

8.   Open resistance persists because everyone knows nothing will be done about it anyway

Supporters:

1.   This is different. He's not solving the problem. I think he wants me to solve them or get those close to the action to solve it. This makes me a little nervous, but it makes sense.

2.   Makes me nervous in that what he is asking makes perfect sense. I feel like I should have had the facts before I came to blame him.

3.   He's a real person and I like that because I feel like I can talk to him and not feel stupid

4.   Wow. I really appreciate the honesty. Now I know what I am working with. It's

uncomfortable, but not knowing is infinitely worse.

5.   I love it when I am encouraged to take initiative to changes that will benefit the whole. I am encouraged by others who take the lead and I get the benefit of their initiative and I want to do the same for others

6.   It is reassuring to know that people will do what they say. My self-esteem grows as I am able to follow through and do what I say here.

7.   Customers regularly thank us with repeat business and let us know they appreciate who we are

8.   He's really committed to this plan. If anything gets in the way either we can count on him to either remove it or help us figure out how we can remove it

9.   I now understand why he took that action he made it clear how this aligns to what we are trying to get done. He's dead serious about what we are trying to accomplish and means I like the conviction.

Peter Drucker, the father of management thinking and author of The Effective Executive: The Definitive Guide to Getting the Right Things Done, The Practice of Management and many more

"'The entrepreneur always searches for change, responds to it, and exploits it as an opportunity."

"Follow effective action with quiet reflection. From the quiet reflection will come even more effective action."

"The most important thing in communication is hearing what isn't said."

"Management is doing things rights; leadership is doing right things."

"If you want something new, you have to stop doing something old"

"Every organization must be prepared to abandon everything it does to survive in the future."

"What gets measured gets managed."

"People in any organization are always attached to the obsolete - the things that should have worked but did not, the things that once were productive and no longer are."

"The leaders who work most effectively, it seems to me, never say "I." And that's not because they have trained themselves not to say "I." They don't think "I." They think "we"; they think "team." They understand their job to be to

224Sustaining profits and doing the right thing!

make the team function. They accept responsibility and don't sidestep it, but "we" gets the credit. This is what creates trust, what enables you to get the task done."

"Most of what we call management consists of making it difficult for people to get their work done."

"If there is any one secret of effectiveness, it is concentration. Effective executives do first things first and they do one thing at a time."

W. Edwards Deming, the dean of American management who lead the Japanese to great success.

> "...a person and an organization must have goals, take actions to achieve those goals, gather evidence of achievement, study and reflect on the data and from that take actions again. Thus, they are in a continuous feedback spiral toward continuous improvement. This is what 'Kaizen' means."

> "What we need to do is learn to work in the system, by which I mean that everybody, every team, every platform, every division, every component is there not for individual competitive profit or recognition, but for contribution to the system as a whole on a win-win basis."

> "Quality is pride of workmanship."

> "Does experience help? NO! Not if we are doing the wrong things."

> "Quality is everyone's responsibility."

> "Eliminate numerical quotas, including Management by Objectives."

> "It is not necessary to change. Survival is not mandatory."

> "Nothing happens without personal transformation."

Sustaining profits and doing the right thing!

"The average American worker has fifty interruptions a day, of which seventy percent have nothing to do with work."

"A bad system will beat a good person every time."

"If you can't describe what you are doing as a process, you don't know what you're doing."

"If you do not know how to ask the right question you discover nothing."

"All anyone asks for is a chance to work with pride."

"Profit in business comes from repeat customers, customers that boast about your project or service, and that bring friends with them."

"Eighty-five percent of the reasons for failure are deficiencies in the systems and process rather than the employee. The role of management is to change the process rather than badgering individuals to do better."

"It is important that an aim never be defined in terms of a specific activity or method. It must always relate   to a better life for everyone."

"Our prevailing system of management has destroyed our people. People are born with intrinsic motivation, self-respect, dignity, curiosity to learn, joy in learning. The forces of destruction begin with toddlers — a prize for the best Halloween costume, grades in school, gold stars — and on up through the university. On the job, people, teams, and divisions are ranked, reward for the top, punishment for the bottom. Management by objectives, quotas, incentive pay, business plans, put together separately, division by division, cause further loss, unknown and unknowable.

"The most valuable "currency" of any organization is the initiative and creativity of its members. Every leader has the solemn moral responsibility to develop these to the maximum in all his people. This is the leader's highest priority."

"A system must be managed. It will not manage itself."

"Rational behavior requires theory. Reactive behavior requires only reflex action."

"It does not happen all at once. There is no instant pudding."

"It only takes a little innovation."

"You should not ask questions without knowledge."

"Any manager can do well in an expanding market."

"In God we trust; all others bring data."

"Adopt a new philosophy of cooperation (win-win) in which everybody wins."

"There is no substitute for knowledge."
"Whenever there is fear, you will get wrong figures."

228 Sustaining profits and doing the right thing!

Dr. Shigeo Shingo, co-creator of the Toyota Production System, author of **A Study of the Toyota Production System: From an Industrial Engineering Viewpoint (Produce What Is Needed, When It's Needed),**

"A relentless barrage of 'why's' is the best way to prepare your mind to pierce the clouded veil of thinking caused by the status quo. Use it often."

"The best approach is to dig out and eliminate problems where they are assumed not to exist."

"Are you too busy for improvement? Frequently, I am rebuffed by people who say they are too busy and have no time for such activities. I make it a point to respond by telling people, look, you'll stop being busy either when you die or when the company goes bankrupt."

"Even the greatest idea can become meaningless in the rush to judgement. To gauge an idea as feasible we must cut our ties to the status quo and find the balance between constructive criticism and judgment. Within that balance we will uncover crucial input for making our ideas a reality."

"The most dangerous kind of waste is the waste we do not recognize."

"It's only the last turn of a bolt that tightens it - the rest is just movement."

"Unless you change direction, you will end up where you are headed."

"We have to grasp not only the Know-How but also 'Know Why', if we want to master the Toyota Production System."

"When you buy bananas all you want is the fruit not the skin, but you have to pay for the skin also. It is a   waste. And you the customer should not have to pay   for the waste."

"Improvement usually means doing something that we have never done before."

"There are four purposes of improvement: easier, better, faster and cheaper. These four appear in the order of priority."

"Those who are not dissatisfied will never make any progress"

230Sustaining profits and doing the right thing!

Taiichi Ohno, VP of Production at Toyota and co-creator of the Toyota Production System and author of Today and Tomorrow

"Having no problems is the biggest problem of all."

"The Toyota style is not to create results by working hard. It is a system that says there is no limit to people's creativity. People don't go to Toyota to 'work' they go there to 'think'."

"Costs do not exist to be calculated. Costs exist to be reduced.
"

"The slower but consistent tortoise causes less waste and is more desirable than the speedy hare that races ahead and then stops occasionally to doze. The Toyota Production System can be realized only when all the workers become tortoises."

"The only place that work and motion are the same thing is the zoo where people pay to see the animals move around"

"If you are going to do kaizen continuously you've got to assume that things are a mess. Too many people just assume that things are all right the way they are. Aren't you guys convinced that the way you're doing things is the right way? That's no way to get anything done. Kaizen is about changing the way things are. If you assume that things are all right the way they are, you can't do kaizen. So, change something!"

"Progress cannot be generated when we are satisfied with existing situations."

"Where there is no Standard there can be no Kaizen"

"All we are doing is looking at the timeline, from the moment the customer gives us an order to the point when we collect the cash. And we are reducing the timeline by reducing the non-value adding wastes."

"Data is of course important in manufacturing, but I place the greatest emphasis on facts."

"Make your workplace into showcase that can be understood by everyone at a glance. In terms of quality, it means to make the defects immediately apparent. In terms of quantity, it means that progress or delay, measured against the plan, and is made immediately apparent. When this is done, problems can be discovered immediately, and everyone can initiate improvement plans."

"No one has more trouble than the person who claims to have no trouble"

"The more inventory a company has, the less likely they will have what they need."

"Ask 'why' five times about every matter."

"We are doomed to failure without a daily destruction of our various preconceptions."

"My first move as the manager of the machine shop was to introduce standardized work."

232 Sustaining profits and doing the right thing!

"If you are going to do TPS you must do it all the way. You also need to change the way you think. You need to change how you look at things."

"Standards should not be forced down from above but rather set by the production workers themselves."

"And we are reducing the timeline by reducing the non-value adding wastes."

"Also, bad quality causes big disruptions in my river system."

"It takes great effort to follow the rules of a pull system ... thus a half-hearted introduction of a pull system brings a hundred harms and not a single gain."

"I'm proud to be Japanese and I wanted my country to succeed. I believed my system was a way that could help us become a modern industrial nation. That is why I had no problem with sharing it with other Japanese companies, even my biggest competitors."

"The key to the Toyota Way and what makes Toyota stand out is not any of the individual elements…But what is important is having all the elements together as a system. It must be practiced every day in a very consistent manner, not in spurts."

Kazuo Inamori, started Kyocera and DDI and led Japan Airlines out of bankruptcy

"Too many people think only of their own profit. But business opportunity seldom knocks on the door of self-centered people. No customer ever goes to a store merely to please the storekeeper."

"The most important thing for the company was to conduct research and development and introduce new, creative, innovative products to compete. To make all the employees happy, we have to have new products [based on] creative ideas."

"It is time to change the motivation system from greed towards money to other ways," he says. "I didn't want to be a rich person. My motivation has been making the people around me happy."

It may sometimes appear that the only people who succeed are those who step on others to get ahead, but this is not true. As shown by proverbs from around the world that emphasize the importance of humility, truly successful people are those who remain humble.

We should be mindful of our human potential to become arrogant without even realizing it, which often happens as soon as things start going well in life and at work.

There are many people, unfortunately, who achieved great success when they were younger, only to begin tumbling downward toward ruin later in life. This is because they forgot their humility and diverged onto the wrong path. Please never forget this principle to "remain humble," even

234Sustaining profits and doing the right thing!

when you become successful as the result of striving harder than anyone else.

The Six Endeavors are essential principles to apply at the office and at home every day:

1.   Strive harder than anyone else

2.   Reflect daily

3.   Do good deeds and serve others

4.   Remain humble

5.   Appreciate life

6.   Don't dwell on the past

Kazuyoshi Hisano, President of Conoway Co., Ltd.,
Professional coach. Lecturer at Temple University for Adults
(Cognitive Psychology / Coaching)

Norman: Kazuyoshi Hisano, I have been teaching the
Harada Method for the past ten years. It has proven to be
very effective helping people to set and attain goals. I feel
that you have advanced this process enormously and I want
to thank you for this interview. You are the author of three
very interesting and important books: *"Gold Vision," "Feed
Forward to Nurture Subordinates Who Always Produce
Results,"* and your latest *"CEO Coaching Theory of Thinking
and Action to Increase Annual Sales by 100 Times."* We
intend to translate the books from Japanese and publish
them in English.

The title of your new book "CEO Coaching .... 100 Times" is
very enticing. Please tell us about your work.

Hisano: My CEO coaching is a service that I can deliver to
top management, to heads of corporations or heads of
divisions. The reason my approach is very effective is that it
has worked very well and is also backed by cognitive
psychology or cognitive science - the latest findings on how
our brain and our mind works. I know that you are currently
reading Lou Tice's book "Personal Coaching for Results,"
ideas he generated around 40 years ago. His ideas were
implemented into the military and the Olympics, people
doing something extreme and it grew and evolved over time.
I found his ideas in Japan around 10 years ago, and I also
learned personally from him. He passed away in 2012.

236Sustaining profits and doing the right thing!

I developed something new basic based on Lou Tice's approach. It is based on science and has proven to be very effective with top management and also works for everybody. The reason people love my approach is because it is very simple. I clearly identify three or four things that we should focus on.

My approach is backed and supported by cognitive science (how the brain works.) I have been coaching actually since I was a child. I will be 46 this week. I love to support other people. I feel very happy when I see somebody becoming successful.

"Our present thoughts determine our future." Lou Tice

Norman: Could you explain how you use cognitive science? (Cognitive science encompasses the traditional disciplines of psychology, computer science, neuroscience, anthropology, linguistics and philosophy. The goal of cognitive science is to understand the principles of intelligence with the hope that this will lead to better comprehension of the mind and of learning and to develop intelligent devices.) (From Wikipedia)

Hisano: Cognitive science research started in the 1950s with the birth of AI, artificial intelligence, sort of both sides of the same coin. People wanted to create something like an AI; to do that the researchers and professors needed to know how our brain works. AI is a like a computer that's tries to copy the workings of our brain. They needed to know how the brain works; how we are recognizing the things that is happening outside, our cognitive awareness, and tried to program all that into a computer. And then it became an AI. These are like both tires of the motorcycle.

These two things cognitive science and artificial intelligence improve together. It matured in 1980s and 1990s, being used in many areas. It took more than 20 years to become a more general technology - understood and applied in the late 20th century. I'm applying the concept to human beings. Simply stated our cognitive system does not allow us to hold two things at the same time.

Two famous examples - what do you see?

If you focus on your goals side, you will not be able to maintain your status quo. We have a born tendency to maintain the status quo, we live in our "comfort zone," because that is reasonable and safe, allowing us to survive as an animal. Animals do not like or need to change. If they have been eating a carrot, they should eat the carrot tomorrow or a year from now. But with people it is different because we have improved our brains and are willing to try to do new things. We can imagine and dream, having a very strong goal. If you have a clear vivid goal, believing the future has already been attained then your brain would see that the goal side is real. This is widely known. If you do image training, focusing on a highly successful vivid future, your cognitive system will start to work so that you will be able to achieve that.

238Sustaining profits and doing the right thing!

It is something simple and people who have been successful know that, but most people do not know that. If you have a goal and if you have a clear vision of that goal, it becomes true. Unfortunately, most people do not know or practice this. Even people in executive position do not necessarily know how to do this. They just work hard. I help them understand how the brain mechanism works for everybody; how it can work for them and how they can use it with their employees or team. It will help you grow your organization and also help to grow your career.

Norman: Thank you, very nice. Please talk also about self-efficacy.

Hisano: We define self-efficacy as a concept, a trust in yourself, confidence in the ability to exert control over one's own motivation, behavior, and social environment and that you can achieve your own goal. It is confidence in yourself; but it's not just confidence that you can achieve your current tasks, it's about the confidence in your future. I believe that a person who has a high self-efficacy thinks that she can achieve her own goal would likely do the right thing. The reason they do not is because they don't have the confidence or more specifically self-efficacy towards achieving their own goal. If you think you can, you can do it. You should be able to get close to that, whether you achieve or not may take time. I believe that the person who has something that he wants to do, and he is working diligently towards will achieve it. This could be applied to the corporation as well. If a corporation has a definitive target goal, a vivid dream, a very big vision and they think that they can do it, they give themselves a wonderful chance of succeeding.

If they have high self-efficacy, a trust in themselves, the

probabilities that they would do right thing becomes higher. And if don't think, if they don't think that they can achieve that or win in a market, the likeliness that they do something wrong becomes higher. I do explain this in my book.

Norman: I have been very lucky in my life without having any real goals. I was never taught to have goals when I was younger. Most people are never taught to have goals when they go to school. You just take life as it comes and just do what you are asked to do. It is wonderful when the corporation gets a great vision and shares that vision with their employees to give each person a new purpose, to get them excited about something good and also allows them to align their own personal goals. When they feel that self-efficacy, that they are serving a higher vision, the company and society benefits.

The average person gets thousands of thoughts a day and it is difficult to follow the best thought. I feel that if I could quiet my mind a little, I could find something else inside me to listen to. I call it the intuitive or higher self that really inspires me in my life. My problem is to make the distinction between the thoughts in my head and the inspiration that comes from above me.

Hisano: We use this concept which we call levels of abstraction. How abstract it is! When I coach CEOs, I ask them to think from a higher position. It does require a ladder of abstraction. Basically, people think in their own layer, in their own world. But when you try to climb the ladder or levels of abstraction leading to an unknown world you force yourself to think in a higher position then something does come from outside of your real world or comfort zone. I call this inspiration or a flash idea. It's hard to explain.

Sustaining profits and doing the right thing!

But you don't know well how it came, but it somehow came. Actually, it was kind of brought through your brain. It feels to you that it didn't come from inside of you, but it came from outside. Every day I talk to myself trying to find out something that is coming from outside of myself. Like it is coming from the space. We can talk more about this later.

If you learn how to develop and use your intuition properly, your brain will give you the right answer. Its correctness is defined by "goals", "efficacy" and "cause".

In other words, if the "goal" is set appropriately, if the self-evaluation "efficacy" is high and the "cause" is strong, the brain will understand the world to be realized, and the brain will help them make the right decisions for the world.

I believe to make the right decision it is better to use your intuition rather than thinking. Of course, studying a lot and thinking a lot are necessary to sharpen that "intuition", so learning and thinking is not a waste. It is an intuition after learning and thinking that helps managers make the right decision.

The idea that looking at the future and working on the future rather than the past and present can create more value, results and happiness.

Kazuyoshi Hisano's new book "CEO coaching..."

◆ A leader is not a consultant but a coach. A consultant is a "solver of a problem" who will consult whenever a new problem arises. A coach is a person who helps me to solve the problem. If you learn the right coaching, you can set goals and solve problems on your own. Leaders bring out the best from their associates - this is specialized coaching. Organizations need to solve problems and achieve their goals. This does require management knowledge and experience.

◆ Leaders need a state-of-the-art coaching method based on cognitive science.

◆ The book provides a practical explanation of the "seven powers" that embody the role for successful management, looking at the common cases of mistakes of leaders.

Sustaining profits and doing the right thing!

Paul Akers, CEO FastCap - 1-888-443-3748

Norman: Thank you very much for doing this.

Paul: How old are you?

Norman: 87, how is your mother?

Paul: You're kicking ass. She's 94 and I'm going to tell you right now at 87 your about 10 times better than her and she's doing great. I'm completely blown away. You are agile, spry and alert.

Norman: I'm very lucky. Larry Fink, CEO Blackrock, is a catalyst for change and inspired me to write this new book. He has demanded that American industry become socially responsible and 181 CEO's from the top American corporations have agreed and have jointly committed to better customer service, to developing their employees, to improving their relationship with their suppliers, and to look at their communities much closer.

Now, the challenge, of course, is for those companies to become more socially responsible and also, I am sure, to not reduce their profits. My book is geared towards offering them options to do it and not lose profits. Problem is if I make a new commitment to develop my employees and I have to invest in them and add value to the company, it might not be done this quarter. It might require a long-term approach to change. Are they, are they willing to sacrifice that time? I don't know. That's a challenge for them.

Paul: The first thing I want to say is, as a successful businessperson that makes good profit, the most important thing is that making only money will never satisfy you. You will dump money down a hole till you're blue in the face, and you will never feel content as a human being. No matter how much you make.

The key is to make profit so that you can live a good life and have flexibility.

It is more important that you have the resources to invest in developing other people because it is the development of other people and seeing other human beings flourish that will give you the true satisfaction that every human being is really looking for. So, this is my epiphany in just 60 seconds.

Norman: Wonderful. That is the challenge. There are greedy billionaires out there.

Paul: You and I, Norman, go back and forth on this subject. All the people I know, and I know billionaires all over the world, they're all incredibly a generous and altruistic. We don't need to look any further than our mutual friend Venu Srinivasan, chairman of TVS Motor who is a billionaire and gives away millions and millions of dollars. He has uplifted over 3.4 million people out of poverty. I don't know those greedy entrepreneurs that most people say are out there, I'm sure they're there. There's no question that they're statistically. They have to be there. What I do know is hundreds, if not thousands of entrepreneurs that are dedicated to not only making money so they can have a sustainable organization, but also into investing in their society and the people that work for them and their customer base. So, this is my paradigm that I live in.

Norman: Yes, this is true. Thank you. But most of these large corporations has focused solely on profits in the last 50 years. This new commitment is a huge shift because they have not invested very much in people development. They have not invested in their people the way they did in the past. For example, General Electric and ATT were known to have greatly invested in their people, which was superb. Look at Bell labs. They made enormous investments in developing new innovations and they virtually disappeared for the short-term view.

Paul: I think if you're a believer in evolution, then you believe its survival of the fittest. And part of having a sustainable future is understanding that you can't just go after profit because it will eventually vanquish your efforts. I don't worry about those greedy capitalists because their days are numbered. It is the laws of nature, it's evolution at its best. It's an unsustainable model. So, I don't spend a lot of time personally rubbing my hands together and saying, oh my gosh, we have this huge problem. I spend all my time setting an example on what good entrepreneurship looks like so that others can follow in my path.

Maybe not the answer you're looking for, but that's my position. I think the real answer is not in the hand ringing about the direction our society or culture going necessarily, but the celebration of all the thousands of thousands of entrepreneurs and capitalists around the world that are doing awesome work. And I could just sit here and go through one after another for you. And that's ultimately what you want, right? Ultimately what you want is for the entrepreneur, the businessperson, and the corporation to act with benevolence towards their fellow man.

Norman: I see customer service with large corporations is terrible. Pick up the phone, they give you a computer to talk to. It's very hard to speak to the person to help you. Companies are concerned about their own productivity not yours.

Paul: I agree too. But I look at it differently. I agree. It's terrible. I, I encounter it almost on a daily basis, but I don't worry about it because if someone's going to eat their lunch, some upstarts going to realize, you can't treat a customer that way. And before long, these people are going to be on the run. A great example that you brought up Bell Laboratories. That's exactly what happened with, ATT.

Norman: For the past 50 years large corporations have been solely going after profits. Many of them have done a great job. Gratefully, they now realize they can't continue to do this anymore. We have to make this dynamic shift if we're going to survive.

Paul: I say evolution, we don't have to make any dynamic shift. Evolution will take care of them. I don't want to help them because the minute we try to act like God but we're not, we're not God. We're not all knowing. We don't know exactly where to apply the pressure and exactly the right time, but you know who the customer is.

Sustaining profits and doing the right thing!

Norman: Let's go back now. I want to talk a little bit about what you've done so well and having the kind of rapport with your customers that helped you create 800 new products.

Paul: First there is no "Fire Wall" to get to me. Anyone can call me. Simply go to the website and my cell phone number is posted. There is no friction to access Paul Lakers. That's the first step. The second step says, if you want us give Paul an idea, it's simple. Take your iPhone, your Google, your Android, whatever version you have and take a video horizontally. Tell me who you are and tell me or show me your idea in about 60 seconds to two minutes. Then send it to my WhatsApp number, which is my cell phone number. Again, total access. And I get that in real time. I watch it and I respond back immediately and let them know my opinion and whether or not I think it's viable for the market. It's so simple. No paperwork. No secretaries needed.

Norman: Okay. What's the next step. How do you decide if the idea is viable and then what?

Paul: That's a very good question, Norman. So, if I think it's viable, the next step is I get their permission to send it to my beta testers. I have probably about 30 beta testers all over North America, Canada and the U S who are professional woodworkers. They are either teachers, woodworkers, cabinetmakers, contractors, finished carpenters, a whole variety of different genres that sit in, but all in our industry, woodworking. Using WhatsApp, I just forward the video and I say, give me your opinion. Grade it a one, two or three: a one, I've got to have it right now. That is all they type is a single digit. I've got to have it right now. How much is it? I want to buy it. Two, Okay. I think it's cool and it's a good idea.

Three, don't waste your time. I have that answer within 10 minutes of the inventor contacting me and then I send those replies back to the inventor, so they know exactly what they think. If it's a one, then it's got my attention and I'm interested in development. If they say two, I'm not interested. If they say it's a three, I'm definitely not interested. If someone's willing to open their wallet then we know we have a winner; then you know you have something unique. The process is that simple.

If I get that response back, then I have them send me the product and I take it to my engineering staff, and we take a look at designing it better. Then my product engineers will design it and 3D print it. We'll look at it, evaluate it, and then when we get a model that we think is good, we send it back to the inventor. We just sent one back yesterday, the most amazing product ever. I mean a product that we're going to sell millions of it. We sent it back to the inventor. The inventor probably will get it on Monday. He'll look at it and say, yep, it's exactly what I thought, or change this and we'll make any little changes and then we'll begin to cut steel or make injection molds or whatever is required to make that product. And then within about three months we'll have a product on the market and that's how simple it is.

Norman: Do you give anything financially?

Paul: Yes, a 5% royalty on the sales price.

Norman: Years ago, I was easily able to reach around 50 CEOs to keynote my conferences, but today, it is almost impossible for me to find their telephone, even the telephone of their secretary.

Paul: That's to their demise. That's evolution. You can get me, which means I'm going to survive. You can't get them. Which means their days are numbered. Their competition is going to eat their lunch. We saw what Southwest airlines did to American airlines and United Delta and everyone else. Southwest airlines was agile and listened to their customers and gave them what they want, and the rest is history. The most successful airline in history.

I don't worry about it and stuff because they're all going to get their lunch, eat.

You can only feed the hungry. You cannot feed someone who's not hungry. If they're not hungry, I don't waste my time with them. I only feed the hungry.

Norman: That's the reason I'm writing the book because they have said that they are willing to make a significant shift from profits to become more socially responsible and I want to show them how to become socially responsible.

Paul: I think the best thing is to show them an example. You know, one of the most important things I ever learned in Japan was Japanese children learn by watching their fathers back. They learn by watching, not by someone instructing them exactly how to do it. Your actions speak louder than anything else and so people learn by showing, not by teaching.

Norman: Yes. Wonderful. I have a lot to learn.

Paul: My passion for Japan was basically channeled through you. You, you taught me to love and appreciate them. I give you the credit for that. Even though initially I didn't quite agree with you on many things, but now I've come to see the light, just like you're going to come to see the light, that evolution will take care of these little entrepreneurs that are greedy.

Norman: What do you say to CEO's in light of this new commitment so that they could take it seriously: to make the profits that they want and also become socially responsible at the same time.

Paul: Do you want to have a great life? Do you want to go into work every day with a smile on your face? You want to go home, tapping the steering wheel happy about what you've accomplished in the people that you work with on a daily basis. It's very simple. Realize that the development of your people, will give you exactly that and if you develop your people vigorously, the profits will come because the profits are not the target. They're the byproduct of a mature, well-developed organization.

Norman: Yes, you're a wonderful man. Paul. I admire you very much. I'm happy to be your friend.

Paul: I'm happy that I got to know you. I'm happy that we were such good friends. I'm happy of all I've

250 Sustaining profits and doing the right thing!

learned from you about Japan and being passionate about what the Japanese have accomplished. It's pretty, it's an amazing journey.

A Leader's Guide for Social Responsibility
The World Needs More Servant Leaders

by **Christophe Makni,** VP Head of Processes, Basler Kantonalbank, Basel, Switzerland

Motivation

Let's start with a short exercise: please reflect about your past experiences for a minute and answer the following two questions:

1. How many teachers and professors did you have at school and at college who deeply had an impact on you and helped you discover your vocation or passion?
2. How many bosses in your entire career made you feel happy, safe and very motivated at your workplace so that you came home every evening deeply satisfied?

Now try to focus on these very few leaders and reflect why they were so much different from the vast majority of all teachers and managers you had in your life. This is one way to look at what is known as "servant leadership" – a way of leading by focusing on people (by "serving" people) which has a huge impact on people's lives and happiness as well as on company culture and business results.

Traditional management

In most companies, management is still very traditional, based on old "command and control" practices. You can see that almost everywhere. In lots of hospitals the staff is overstressed and miserable, and so many nurses and doctors end up burnt out. The same pattern repeats everywhere: focus on cost cutting, firing staff to satisfy

Sustaining profits and doing the right thing!
shareholders, advertising for nice values and products but doing the opposite, micromanagement… you name it. The consequences are already well known and documented: disengaged staff, yearly increase of the number of burn outs etc. Traditional command and control practices do not seem to be adequate anymore.

What is Servant Leadership?

Servant leadership is about serving others as a leader on the path of achieving a great mission altogether. You place the focus on the people, and you serve them as a leader - yes you "serve" them. it is about the others. And the others working together in a chain of mutual support can really change the company's culture and even the world - way more than you could alone.

This applies in a business context but also in your community, family, sports club etc. It is a leadership concept and a mindset which is extremely powerful and unlocks the potential of people. Very few leaders know about it and apply it in their day to day lives. As a transformative leader you will be able to reach your next development level if you are working on your servant leadership mindset and attitude. If you want to become a true Lean or Agile Leader, and you truly care about people, servant leadership is part of your developmental journey. And yes, it is absolutely possible to lead and serve people at the same time…

By creating a culture of serving others, your reports will start copying you and doing the same, their reports as well... Over time you start rolling out a culture of support and at this point of time everything becomes possible. Imagine just for a second what it would feel like when all your colleagues at the workplace would be delighted to support you every day to help you move forwards in your projects - no internal obstacles, no internal politics, no escalation, no conflicts anymore .... how does that feel? Well it is your responsibility as a leader to ignite this little flame of serving others and making it a daily practice - and over time it will grow to a happiness fire rolling out through your entire organization.

Impact on people

Most people spend the majority of their time at work. Traditional managers tend to demotivate or even worse scare people. Restoring safety and happiness at the workplace must be our goal as a leader - and this has a positive impact on the creativity and productivity of the people. One great example of a CEO working exactly on this is Rich Sheridan (author of two great books: "Joy, Inc. – how we built a workplace people love" and "Chief Joy officer".). Another great example is Paul Akers, CEO of FastCap, who invests his entire energy into building a fantastic Lean culture as the backbone for a sustainable success and being a true servant leader every day. The only way to combine happiness at the workplace and successful sustainable business results is by deploying a culture of servant leadership among the leaders.

How to start with servant leadership?

Servant leadership really starts with yourself. Ask yourself:

- What is your goal in life?
- What makes you happy?
- What is your passion?
- What are your values?
- How much do you love the people who work for you?

Love for people starts in your heart. You have to consciously decide that you want to re-orient your life serving others. Follow your heart.

In order to change yourself and grow, you need to work daily on your vision and on your life's goal - that includes daily practices and new routines. Reflect at the end of your day: spend at least 20 minutes every evening analyzing your day and defining the main corrective actions for the next day. Try to remain positive and emphasize the positive moments of the day in your mind. Get a coach to help you install these daily practices, getting feedback. You can only be a leader once you have grown personally and worked on yourself at the same time.

Serve others and be authentic - do not expect anything in return. Just do it with your heart. You could compare this pattern to a mother's role, whose goal it is to serve and protect their children in every sense. She eats last, goes last to bed and is the first to stand up in the morning. So does a good leader – he leaves the office when all the others are long gone, he appears first early in the morning and he even cleans up the coffee cups of his employees on the weekend (this last point may sound weird to you now, but let me come back to this story later on).

Work on developing your direct reports by coaching them every day - help them achieve their goals and realize their dreams. We all know many people who are not happy at the workplace and who are not achieving any of their dreams at the end of their life. Isn't it sad? Isn't our responsibility as a leader to guarantee our employee's safety and happiness at the workplace while focusing on creating the maximum value for our customers? As basic as it sounds there are really not a lot of companies and leaders doing that on a daily basis. The impact on respecting your employees and developing them is huge on the customer side. Happy employees interact with their customers in a completely different way than disengaged employees. And this has a positive impact on sales.

How to establish a servant leadership culture

You cannot change your entire company over night, but you can start within your division and invest time and energy coaching your people daily. And you can have a great impact on your reports' happiness at work. Never complain about your organization, always work on yourself and your team and over time your stakeholders and the rest of the organization will notice the difference of mindset in your division.

Of course, in "servant leadership" the "leadership" part is essential - you need to act and behave like leader, so that people feel it is right to follow you. It is your responsibility to:

- set a clear vision, goals and objectives
- live and respect the defined values
- engage with your teams to work on the common vision

But you do not force people to do what you tell them; you inspire them by your authentic passion to the point where they want to make your dream their dream as well. When this happens, you have a magic connection to your team, and everything gets possible. And when issues arise, you know that everybody will give their best to solve them.

How I learned about Servant Leadership

Sustaining profits and doing the right thing!

As a young manager I developed my standard practices based on common management practices: setting performance objectives, tracking with metrics, motivating and pushing my reports, giving feedback... I was never attracted by the paperwork related to the management job (like reporting or filling out forms) but was more attracted by the people development side.

As I discovered the Japanese Management practices and studied Lean more than 10 years ago, I was really amazed to discover the stories of some Japanese CEOs who start the day by cleaning the toilets of their companies. Honestly at that time I did not get the point. I understood the impact of that much later. This is already a sign of servant leadership but is only the tip of the iceberg. The concept is called the "upside-down pyramid" (with the broader base on the top): customers are at the top of the pyramid, then come added value workers and then the management at the bottom. The management's only job is to support workers to please customers. You can reflect yourself to see whether you have a standard pyramid where the management sits at the top or this upside-down pyramid mindset in your company.

What it means for me today

Servant Leadership today has transformed the way I lead. I first try to understand the goal of my direct reports so that I can better help them reach their goals. I use the Harada Method daily which is a very good helping me come up with an ambitious goal and an action plan to reach it. Servant Leadership means having strong values like respecting people and focusing on developing them and producing high quality results for the customers.

Additionally, it is about:

1.   Giving everything every day
1.   Investing time and energy in developing and coaching my people
2.   Supporting my direct reports whatever happens
3.   Creating a family mindset at the workplace – that to me is even stronger than a team spirit
4.   Serving others: Helping others gives a good feeling and sets clear signs - the higher you are in the hierarchy the more you need to spend time serving others

Cleaning dishes

At this point I would like to share with you a little story about "cleaning up coffee cups" that I already mentioned above.

From time to time I come to my office during the weekend to finish the unfinished work from the busy week and to plan the coming week. After doing so, something attracted my attention: every weekend I found at least three dirty coffee cups (with some remaining cold coffee inside) on the table of one of my reports. So, I started as a routine to clean up her cups and desk each Saturday and on Monday morning she would always find a clean table. If you think that she was going to thank me for doing that, you are wrong – she did not even notice a thing. And I decided not to say anything. After all I just wanted to do her a small favor so that she feels better when she starts the week on Monday morning with a clean table. However, one day while we were having a cup of coffee in the kitchen, she drank only half of her coffee and I couldn't contain myself of telling her that this seemed to be the normal way of how she drinks her coffee. "How do you know about that?", she asked. I told her that I have been cleaning up her cups of

Sustaining profits and doing the right thing!
coffee with remaining coffee inside on her table during the weekend for a couple of months now. She was really surprised since she had never experienced a former boss in her life who took care of his reports in this way…

This might seem just like a little good and friendly gesture, but in the context of my five principles above it punctuates the meaning of "creating a family mindset at the workplace" and "serving others".

And it definitely had one more positive side effect: thenceforth I never found any coffee cups anymore on her table.

Servant Leadership metrics

You can have a feeling of how you are doing as a servant leader by getting the feedback from a coach (if you are actively working on yourself then you most probably have one) and of the people working closely with you. Observe especially the following aspects:

- How many people come to you each month to tell you that you inspire them?
- How many people told you that you helped them change their lives?
- How many people told you that they once cried for joy while going home after work?

If the answer is zero for each of those questions you still have some work to do on your personal development and leadership skills before you can call yourself a true servant leader.

Conclusion

Be the leader you dream to have. Stop complaining and be positive. Give everything every day. Focus on your people. Never give up your dreams and help your people realize their dreams. That is servant leadership.

260Sustaining profits and doing the right thing!

Summary

"Despite the fact that Millennials are coming of age in one of the most difficult economic climates in the past 100 years, a recent Nielsen global online study found that they continue to be most willing to pay extra for sustainable offerings—almost three-out-of-four respondents in the latest findings..." - https://tinyurl.com/rvpzzrs

As you read this book, I hope that the coronavirus has been fully contained and that we can rebuild the world in a more positive way. The virus has been a tragedy with many lives lost, many lives disrupted. Try to look at it as if the "earth," was shouting at us to change our behavior. If we continued doing the same things we were doing, the world would not continue to exist: air pollution is killing over 8 million each year, the seas are rising, the earth's temperature is hotter, plastics are paralyzing our oceans and financial inequities are probably higher than ever before.

Our new thrust to become more socially responsible is a powerful beginning to bring positive change to our organizations and to the world. Believe in your employees and yourself that you can do it. You can make things right.

I thank you all.

INDEX